MICROTEACHING IN TEACHER EDUCATION AND TEACHING

Microteaching in Teacher Education & Training

Brian McGarvey and Derek Swallow

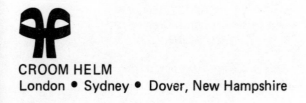

CROOM HELM
London • Sydney • Dover, New Hampshire

© 1986 Brian McGarvey and Derek Swallow,
Croom Helm Ltd, Provident House, Burrell Row,
Beckenham, Kent, BR3 1AT

Croom Helm Australia Pty Ltd, Suite 4, 6th Floor,
64-76 Kippax Street, Surry Hills, NSW 2010, Australia

British Library Cataloguing in Publication Data

McGarvey, Brian
    Microteaching in teacher education and
    teaching. — (New patterns of learning
    series)
    1. Microteaching
    I. Title   II. Swallow, Derek   III. Series
    370′.7′33   LB1731
    ISBN 0-7099-4613-9

Croom Helm, 27 South Main Street,
Wolfeboro, New Hampshire 03894-2069, USA

Library of Congress Cataloging-in-Publication Data

McGarvey, Brian, 1936-
    Microteaching in teacher education and training.

    Bibliography: p.
    Includes index.
    1. New University of Ulster — Curricula — History —
20th century. 2. Microteaching — Case studies.
I. Swallow, Derek, 1946-   . II. Title.
LB2226.C656M35 1986   370′.7′33   86-13507
ISBN 0-7099-4613-9

Printed and bound in Great Britain by Mackays of Chatham Ltd, Kent

CONTENTS

TO   OLIVE AND ELIZABETH

NEW PATTERNS OF LEARNING

The purpose of this series

This series of books provides an introduction to
trends and areas of current thinking in education.
The books will be of interest to all educators,
trainers and administrators responsible for the
implementation of educational policies in higher,
further and continuing education.
Each book contains extensive references to key
works to enable the reader to pursue selected areas
in more depth should he or she so wish.
This book, "Microteaching in Teacher Education
and Training", was written by Dr. Brian McGarvey and
Dr. Derek Swallow of the Department of Curriculum
Studies, University of Ulster. It is based on their
extensive experience of microteaching both as a
training programme for the development of teaching
skills and as an education programme for the
development of students' understanding of teaching
and of themselves as teachers.
It reviews the developments in microteaching
practice and rationale and reports descriptive
research of microteaching in action. The
interpersonal relationships between students and
supervisors and the nature of students' learning in
microteaching are explored. These descriptions are
used to illustrate established models of
microteaching and to propose a framework of
constructs and dimensions for microteaching.
It is an important book for all those concerned
with the education and training of teachers.

                                        P.J. Hills
                                        Cambridge

ACKNOWLEDGEMENTS

We would like to thank the many students and
supervisors who permitted their microlessons and
review conferences to be observed, who responded to
the range of questionnaires and inventories and who
were very willing to spend considerable time talking
to us about their experiences, beliefs and values.
We would also like to acknowledge the contributions
of colleagues who offered constructive advice at
various stages of the research. In particular,
Gareth Parry, the organising tutor for
microteaching, was extremely helpful in facilitating
the research and Joe Harris made very significant
contributions to the development of the inventories
in the exploratory stages of the research. Others
who provided invaluable support were Don Batts and
Gordon Rae.

Brian McGarvey
Derek Swallow

Chapter 1.

MICROTEACHING

Microteaching is now used very widely as a component of teacher education and training programmes. When it was first introduced it was presented largely as a behaviour modification technique to improve teaching performance and so was emphasising the training aspect in the preparation of teachers. Seidman (1969) argued for its use for education purposes and, as microteaching has spread and its practices have become more diversified, it has moved very considerably in the direction that Seidman advocated.

This book is a contribution to charting the development of microteaching practice and theory and to understanding its potential and flexibility. We report the research into microteaching at the New University of Ulster from 1974 to 1984 and describe the ways in which it has been used in this institution. We link this research to ongoing developments elsewhere, especially in the United Kingdom, and present our understanding of what microteaching is and the various ways in which it can be used.

EARLY DEVELOPMENTS

Teaching is a very complex activity and practising teaching in normal classroom situations is not only a potentially threatening experience for beginning students, but also does not easily provide them with both the feedback about their teaching performance and the time for analytical and reflective thought that are necessary for swift learning gains. Microteaching was first introduced at Stanford University in 1963 (Allen and Ryan, 1969) as a scaled down practice teaching situation in a laboratory setting. It was intended to reduce the complexity of the practice teaching situation and provide a gentler introduction to teaching through learning to teach in a safe, controlled environment. The complex skills of teaching were broken down into simpler, component skills and rating schedules were developed to define and monitor the attributes of each skill. The students attended lectures and skill demonstrations (often videotaped 'models' showing examples of good practice) on these component skills of teaching. The students then practised these skills by preparing and teaching short lessons (5-10 minutes) to small classes (6-8 pupils or peers). They received feedback about their performance by viewing and discussing the videorecording of their microlessons, using rating schedules to guide their analysis of the skills being practised. Practising a specific teaching skill in a short lesson with swift feedback provided a very much shortened learning cycle as compared to conventional teaching practice in classrooms. This meant that students could receive more support and have more information about their performance. They would also have more opportunities for repeat practice and for developing their powers of perception and analysis. Thus microteaching was intended to help students improve their teaching skills and their self-confidence.

Since its introduction there has been a very dramatic growth in the use of microteaching and many different formats have been developed. Within the general framework of microteaching the classes can vary in size and may include school pupils or peers. The lessons can vary in length. The component skills selected for attention may vary, though there has been considerable consensus as to the core of skills to be included. The feedback can be provided by videorecording, audiotaping or being observed live by a tutor, though videorecording has come to be the common mode of feedback. The student may review the videorecording and discuss the teaching performance with a tutor, or with other students, or both, and the teaching may be analysed by using teaching skill rating schedules or a teacher-pupil interaction analysis system or just by discussion of its salient features. In some programmes the student then goes on to modify the approach and reteach the lesson to a different class, with further feedback being provided.

Thus the term microteaching is "generic rather than specific" (Brown, 1975a) and includes a wide range of practices which can be varied as desired to suit local needs and conditions and to reflect the underlying rationale on which its use is founded. It is this great flexibility in use which is one of microteaching's most attractive features.

One example which illustrates the wide range of microteaching strategies has been provided by McGarvey and Williams (1978). They contrasted their uses of microteaching with student science teachers. In the one case the tutor set aside one day to provide four groups of four students each with one session of microteaching lasting one and a half hours. Portable videorecording equipment was set up in the science laboratory and the four students were recorded in turn as they taught five minute lessons to the others in their group. The tutor then took each individual student through their own lesson in separate fifteen minute review sessions. In the other case the science students were part of the year group of some two hundred students who took a twelve week microteaching programme in which each student taught a 10-15 minute lesson every week to a microclass of 6-8 primary school pupils in a suite of special classrooms equipped with CCTV recording facilities. The students in groups of four then reviewed their lessons with their tutor and these viewing and discussion sessions generally lasted about two hours. Both these approaches were believed to be very beneficial to the students.

The growth of microteaching in a variety of formats has resulted in there now being a very extensive literature documenting the various practices that have been used, describing the associated research studies and providing critiques of the underlying assumptions, definitions and theories that have been applied in microteaching. As well as the many studies in the U.S.A., extensive investigations of microteaching have been conducted in Australia, Sweden, Israel and the United Kingdom. In the United Kingdom microteaching for student teachers was pioneered at Stirling University from 1968, at the New University of Ulster from 1969 and at the Ulster Polytechnic from 1971. It was developed for the inservice training of experienced teachers at Lancaster University from 1972 as an adaptation of Borg and colleagues' work (1938) in the U.S.A. on Minicourses. Minicourses were self-instructional microteaching packages each of which focused on a precisely defined teaching skill (e.g. use of discussion questions).

The vast literature on microteaching has been

thoroughly reviewed from time to time in terms of both surveying the practices adopted and summarising the research findings, e.g. Turney et al. (1973a), Brusling (1974), Brown (1975b), and Hargie and Maidment (1979). It will be sufficient for our purpose just to point out the significant generalisations from the research into microteaching and to concentrate on following the way in which the distinctive rationales for microteaching have developed.

There is now plenty of evidence to show that microteaching has been a valuable addition to the repertoire of methods used in teacher education and training. In this respect it is important to remember that microteaching is an additional technique and is not intended as a substitute for school-based experience. Many studies have indicated that microteaching is effective in producing improvements in teaching performance and it has also been found to change perceptions of teaching as well as performance. This seems to be the case because microteaching includes discrimination learning of teaching skills through identifying the skills in action, analysing their components and evaluating their effectiveness in use. In this way the student learns to discriminate between 'appropriate' and 'inappropriate' behaviours (Wagner, 1973). For the actual improvement of teaching skills, microteaching would seem to be more cost and time effective than school-based practice. Students have been found generally to react very positively to their microteaching showing favourable attitudes and valuing their experiences. Performance on microteaching has been found to be a reasonably good predictor of success in classroom teaching.

McIntyre, MacLeod and Griffiths (1977) have commented that much of the research into microteaching has been of the experimental type, comparing different versions of microteaching in order to find the most effective combination of components to optimise students' skill learning. They considered that "in general the outcomes of this considerable body of experimental research have been unenlightening" and argued that this was so because of premature concentration on experimental research designs in circumstances in which experimental research was not being used to test hypotheses derived from cogent theories. They argued that the theoretical understanding of the learning that takes place in microteaching was still

4

under development and that it would be "a more economical research strategy to use looser and more exploratory designs to provide insights from which theoretical ideas could be developed."

Hargie and Saunders (1983a) have supported this view and point out that there is a dearth of valid, reliable research instruments for use in microteaching investigations. Hargie (1980) has also stated "more research is needed in order to investigate not only how microteaching works, but also why microteaching is successful." The researches described in this book are descriptive explorations of tutors' actions and beliefs and of students' reactions and learning within one particular format of microteaching and they include the development of a number of instruments for following the students' attitudes and learning and the interactions of tutors and their students.

TRENDS IN PRACTICE AND RATIONALE

Many of the early criticisms of microteaching, by both practitioners and onlookers, were concerned with its behaviour modification approach to learning to teach (e.g. St.John-Brooks and Spelman, 1973) and with the specific teaching skills which had been isolated as those observable teaching behaviours implied to be basic to effective teaching. Could a complex skill like teaching be learned by dividing it into simpler component skills or behaviours and practising these? What justifications were there on the grounds of research evidence and theoretical frameworks in deeming selected teaching skills to be particularly important? Other criticisms were concerned with the artificial nature of microteaching. It focused more on the separateness of teaching skills than on their combination. It emphasised how to use a particular skill rather than when to use it. It was a laboratory situation which did not simulate actual classroom situations at all closely.

It has been largely as an attempt to respond to these criticisms that the distinctive practices and rationales for microteaching have developed. At this stage of our discussions we shall show how this thinking was developing in the early and mid 1938's in order to set the scene in which our researches were conducted. We shall return to a more detailed discussion of current views on microteaching in the final chapter.

The Behaviour Modification Approach

The initial model of microteaching used at Stanford University scaled down the practice teaching situation and used videorecordings and a rating schedule, the Stanford Teacher Competence Appraisal Guide, to provide feedback about overall teaching performance. Reteach sessions were provided to help improve performance. This system was developed and refined with experience over a number of years and Brusling (1974) has summarised these early developments clearly. The team of workers introduced the component skills approach and defined fourteen technical skills of teaching, which they considered could be applied in many different teaching contexts. Figure 1.1 lists these component skills.

Fig. 1.1: The Stanford Component Skills of Teaching

1. Stimulus variation
2. Set induction
3. Closure
4. Silence and nonverbal cues
5. Reinforcement of student participation
6. Fluency in asking questions
7. Probing questions
8. Higher-order questions
9. Divergent questions
10. Recognising attending behaviour
11. Illustrating and use of examples
12. Lecturing
13. Planned repetition
14. Completeness of communication

These teaching skills were identified largely from the consensus opinions of those involved and, although Allen and Ryan (1969) acknowledged that the educational literature was consulted, no rationale or research evidence was presented to justify the focus on these particular skills. Videotaped models of these teaching skills and feedback rating schedules specific to each skill were introduced to encourage desired changes in students' teaching behaviours. This was the system described by Allen and Ryan (1969) and often referred to as the 'Stanford model'. Another of its originators, McDonald (1973), acknowledged the grounding of this system in behaviour modification theory and pointed out that this included the cognitive understanding of the processes involved as well as the perfection of skills through their separation and practice.

The Behaviour Modification Approach was also strongly emphasised in the Minicourse Model of microteaching developed by Borg and co-workers (1938) at Berkeley University, California for use in the inservice training of teachers. The Minicourse Model has been adopted by a number of institutions including the University of Lancaster (Perrott, 1977). Each Minicourse focused upon precisely defined teaching skills or 'competency clusters', e.g. using questioning skill to promote discussion. The teacher followed the handbook and videotape provided which together explained and showed how to use the skill. Then he practised the skill with some pupils in his own school and videorecorded this microlesson. The videorecording was next viewed critically using self-evaluation forms for guidance. Finally, the lesson was replanned, retaught to another group of children, reviewed and self-evaluated.

The Minicourses were strongly rooted in behaviour modification theory:

> To develop specific teaching skills efficiently..., first, the learner must be given a very clear definition of the specific skills he is to master...(which) should include a visual model or example... Second, the learner must have an opportunity to practise the skill... under simpler and less demanding conditions than those found in full class teaching situations. Third, the learner must receive specific feedback on his practice that will help him to bring his performance close to the model or definition. The Minicourse Instructional Model is designed to supply these three requirements... (Borg et al., 1938, p.27)

Following the introduction of the Minicourses at Lancaster University, an independent evaluator, Applebee (1976), reported his insights into the implementation of the Minicourse Model and the focus on Component Skills and Behaviour Modification Approaches.

> What (the trainee) seems to learn when the skill is emphasised is to choose this skill more frequently in specific instructional situations, supplanting other options previously favoured... The result is sometimes

a distressing distortion of normal teaching...
Some of the practice which teachers get is
practice in teaching poorly, in order to
produce situations where the 'skills' can be
applied. (p.40)

The problem was that objectives centred on
training in specific skills resulted in a course
dedicated to how particular aspects of behaviour
were to be applied, with little attention given to
the appropriate use of these skills or to the
integration of such training into the aims and
complexity of the school classroom. In the final
paragraph of his report, Applebee summarised his
attitude to the Component Skills and Behaviour
Modification Approaches to microteaching on which
the Minicourse Model was based.

The view of teaching which it embodies is too
simplistic, the focus of instruction too
isolated from classroom objectives, the context
too teacher-centred. (p.43)

The following points summarise the range of
criticisms which were made about the Component
Skills and Behaviour Modification Approaches as
exemplified in the Stanford and Minicourse Models.

It was difficult to organise (Salsbury, 1969;
Brown and Armstrong, 1975).

It presented a behaviouristic image of the
world, ignoring the purposes and context of
teaching, while disregarding trainees' values
relating to education and social reform
(Seidman, 1969; Nash and Agne, 1971; Nash,
1972).

It inferred that the sum of the component
skills resulted in good teaching, ignoring the
individual differences in teachers and pupils
whereby teachers employing identical teaching
techniques produce different effects in their
pupils (Seidman, 1969).

It distorted the teaching situation. Students
experienced great difficulty in planning and
executing a lesson designed to demonstrate
particular skills, particularly when the use of
such skills seem unwarranted in the way the
lesson developed. Also, the students found the

constraints of the short lesson very artificial (Foster, Heys and Harvey, 1973; Brown and Armstrong, 1975), and pupils often found the short lesson meaningless in terms of learning gains (Wolfe, 1938; Brusling, 1972).

By focusing on achieving expertise in individual skills it avoided the importance of the integration and assimilation of these behaviours into an individual's personal approach to teaching (Pereira and Guelcher, 1938).

It promoted the display and performance of specified skills, which required thoughtful planning, yet not enough attention was being paid to lesson planning (Waimon, Bell and Ramseyer, 1972). With the focus on skill training, little instruction was being given in the organisation of learning experiences for pupils (Merrill, 1968).

Reservations were expressed about the appropriateness of a technical skills approach for pre-service teachers. Training undergraduates in specific skills may be premature (Kallenbach and Gall, 1969; Foster, Heys and Harvey, 1973).

Cueing trainees on to specific behavioural skills could possibly impede teacher self-confrontation and self-evaluation (Baker, 1938).

Concentrating on the mechanics of teacher behaviour paid little attention to developing insights into the nature of teaching (Schaefer, 1938; Combs, 1972).

Despite these criticisms microteaching spread very rapidly throughout the world. Evidently there were important features and advantages of microteaching which were very attractive. The main attractions were:

The short lesson and small class provided a relatively safe initial learning environment, likened by Hargie (1980) to leading the trainee "gently into the teaching situation rather than throwing him into the deep end hoping he will be able to manage."

It provided a very short learning cycle so that much progress could be made in a way that was both cost and time effective.

Viewing and discussing the videotape was a rich source of feedback for students about themselves, their teaching skills, teaching in general and pupils' characteristics.

It was much more under the control of the training institution than was school-based experience.

What happened was that other institutions were attracted by these advantages, started from the Stanford Model and modified it to meet those particular criticisms that they felt were important.

The Component Skills Approach

Ward (1970) obtained responses to a survey questionnaire from 144 of the 176 secondary teacher education institutions using microteaching in the United States. He found that there was general disinterest in the "technical skills of teaching as defined at Stanford", reflecting the widespread move away from the specifically defined Behaviour Modification Approach, a situation lamented by McDonald (1973):

The most undesirable consequence of the promotion of microteaching was that the role of behaviour modification in training was obscured. (p.73)

This trend was not confined to an American context but also appeared to refer to the majority of early applications of microteaching (Foster, Heys and Harvey, 1973; Brusling, 1974). Hargie and Maidment (1979) surveyed the use of microteaching in the British Isles in 1975 and reported widespread use. 177 of the 220 U.K. institutions approached responded and 113 were using microteaching and 25 were planning to do so. Hargie and Maidment described the systems in use and the ways in which they had been conceived. They reported that the Stanford Model "has survived well enough" but that while developing skills was still the dominant objective, there was also account being taken of the cognitive learning by students about teaching and some recognition of the value of microteaching for affective development. There was a fairly substantial agreement among respondents as to the basic skills, which were still largely those of the Stanford Model. However the Behaviour Modification Approach was not much in evidence and these researchers considered that most microteaching programmes in the United Kingdom were conceived in terms of the social psychology of teaching.

In Sydney University Turney et al. (1973b, 1975, 1976a, 1976b, 1977) had introduced a microteaching system which focused on "specific observable teaching behaviours which seem basic to effective teaching." The skills were regarded as the "meaningful and acquirable parts of a highly complex process" and as such represented "an analysis of the teaching process into discrete well defined behaviours transferable to most classroom situations." What was particularly noteworthy about the 'Sydney Micro Skills' was that selection of the component teaching skills was based on two main criteria - the needs expressed by tutors in Australian teacher education programmes which were implementing microteaching and the checking of these needs against an overview of research and theory on teaching. Turney et al. (1973a) have reported this survey of needs and analysis of relevant research. Thus the component teaching skills which comprised the Sydney programme, listed in Figure 1.2, were justified in terms of both needs and research findings. However, Turney et al. were still careful to point out that "the final validity of the skills has yet to be proved."

Fig. 1.2: The Sydney Micro Skills

Reinforcement
Questioning
Variability
Explaining
Set induction
Closure
Discipline and classroom management
Small group and individualised teaching skills
Skills related to developing pupils' thinking
through discovery learning and creativity

Turney et al. pointed out that, while the influence of the Stanford and Berkeley skill categories were recognisable in this list, there were four groups of skills (small group teaching,

11

developing thinking, individualising teaching,
classroom management and discipline) which were new
and which represented a move away from a narrow
focus on teacher-orientated skills to "more informal
teaching situations centred about the individual
child and his development."

Other special features of the Sydney programme
were that students should understand the research
and theory concerning the skill and be able to
recognise and discriminate the skill. Also, the
microteaching experience had strong links with
practice teaching to help the student transfer the
skill to ordinary classroom situations. In this way
the skills were being used to develop a "practical
and penetrating understanding" of teaching and to
build up an overall teaching ability.

Thus the way microteaching was being taken up
by many institutions showed an acceptance of a
Component Skills Approach with rejection of the
Behaviour Modification Approach. Typically,
microteaching was being used as an opportunity for
controlled practice in a scaled down teaching
situation. The emphasis was being placed on the
progressive integration of skills as opposed to
training in specific skills, with most programmes
containing a gradual increase in complexity from a
simplified encounter to that requiring use of a
variety of skills. Such an approach was often
accompanied by the progressive increase in lesson
time and (in some cases) in the number of pupils in
the microclass, with the intention of facilitating
the transition from microteaching to classroom
experience. Relationships were often sought with
curriculum tutors so that trainees might obtain
practice in the methods particular to their chosen
area of teaching interest and future careers.
However, while the move away from the Behaviour
Modification Approach was being justified in terms
of its limitations, alternative rationales for
microteaching were rarely given and this led
Brusling (1974) to remark:

> The pressing problems of establishing
> strategies of teaching out of a list of
> teaching skills, of recognising the fact that
> skills are not isolated parts of behaviour but
> interact with each other, have yet to be
> solved. (p.105)

The Dynamic Skills Approach
One interesting early case which did offer an

alternative rationale was that developed in the
University of Chicago - the Dynamic Skills Approach.
This approach and its rationale have been described
by Guelcher, Jackson and Necheles (1970) and by
Pereira and Guelcher (1970). They argued that the
Stanford Model largely ignored the relationships
between the skills, their appropriateness and
relevance to the particular teaching situation.
They regarded teaching as a purposeful activity with
the context in which the skills were being practised
also important - i.e. the lesson itself, which had
to be taken into account in order to give students
experience in deciding the appropriateness, level,
and combination of the particular skills deemed
applicable. They asserted that "the basic weakness
in microteaching stemmed from the fact that the
lessons used by the teachers were not sufficiently
thought out" (Guelcher et al, 1970), and they
developed the Dynamic Skills Approach to alleviate
this problem.

The Dynamic Skills Approach considered two
aspects of teaching a lesson - the content and the
behaviours of the teacher. Lesson planning was
emphasised in that the subject matter was viewed as
the context in which the anticipated skills were
practised, so that the skills (e.g. reinforcement,
classroom management) were considered as subsystems
and not as isolated behaviours. The organisers
introduced five stages between the identification
and discrimination of skills (which included
modelling) and the actual teaching of the
microlesson. These stages, which were designed to
improve the skills of lesson planning, were:

the Practicum, in which instruction was given
in the qualities of a good lesson, based on
thorough planning;

peer group microteaching, included to promote
the development of confidence and the skills of
structuring a lesson;

a seminar on the supervision of microteaching,
in which students (as would-be supervisors)
were trained, using previously videotaped
lessons, in isolating those dynamic elements of
the lesson that seemed to account for its
success or failure and applying these elements
to evaluate the behaviours of teacher and
students;

13

a seminar on the nature of skills as "the dynamics of the lesson", in which teaching skills were explained on the basis of their contribution to implementing the logical structure of the lesson;

a pre-teach discussion between tutor and student about the nature of the lesson to be taught and how the teaching skills would be incorporated to achieve the lesson's aims. In this way evaluation criteria were established for application in the later analysis session.

Then followed the actual microteaching session which included the microlesson, its review and discussion and a further reteach cycle.

Thus the rationale underpinning the Dynamic Skills Approach was that of systematic lesson planning based on appropriate subject matter. It stressed that the skills to be practised must be carefully woven into the lesson plan. The student needed to be in control of the lesson's logical structure and content in order to be able to concentrate on the significant interactions between teacher and pupils. In this way the teaching skills could be considered as learning dynamics, promoting those interactions of teacher and pupils deemed necessary to facilitate the logical development of the learning. The teaching skill was given meaning only as a specific teaching behaviour within the context of a particular lesson which had specific learning aims.

The Social Psychological Approach

Microteaching was being introduced into the United Kingdom at a time when several authors were having a critical look at the then current approaches to the training of teachers (Morrison and McIntyre, 1969; Stones and Morris, 1972). These publications proved to be very influential, as evidenced by their frequent citation by others. Morrison and McIntyre argued that:

given adequate theoretical models... many aspects of teaching can be described in ways which lead to a better appreciation of current practice and how it might be improved. (p.13)

In looking at teaching practice Stones and Morris pointed out that its role and objectives needed to be clarified and that redirections were required to forge stronger links between the practice situation and theories of teaching. Both sets of authors saw microteaching as a valuable innovation giving a greater degree of control than normally found in classroom teaching and hence having the potential to emphasise the relationship between theory and practice so that students would learn to "master the teaching model."

Morrison and McIntyre (1969) had noted that "socially competent teachers were more effective in teaching" and in another publication (1972) they drew attention to the social psychological perspective as one way of looking at teaching. This approach viewed teaching as a socially skilled activity dependent upon good interpersonal relationships and communication between teacher and learner. Meanwhile Argyle (1967, 1969a, 1969b) had developed the notion of teaching as a complex social skill. He argued that a teacher interacting with his students was engaging in a socially skilled performance and that the necessary social skills could be acquired in a manner similar to that used for training in motor skills. First the social skills involved in teaching were to be identified and students given training in each skill separately. Then the skills were to be put back together again, integrating them into the overall teaching performance. Argyle (1969b) saw microteaching as a valuable method of helping students practise the social skills of teaching and develop a thorough understanding of the processes of social interaction. These ideas were taken up by Brown (1975b, 1975c) at the New University of Ulster and by Hargie and coworkers (1977, 1978, 1979) at the Ulster Polytechnic as the theoretical framework for their microteaching systems. The component skills of teaching were now being presented as those social skills required for effective interpersonal behaviour, and as such the major skill categories of the original Stanford Model were still retained, e.g. set induction, closure, liveliness, explanation, and questioning. In these microteaching systems improvement in the social skills of teaching was dependent not only on practising the skills but on how well these interpersonal skills were understood and perceived.

Brown developed a model of microteaching which incorporated both the Social Skills Training Model of Argyle and the view of Hirst (1971) that teaching is an intentional activity, the general intention being that pupils will learn. Brown considered that

15

the student teacher had a twofold intention "that his pupils learn while he learns to teach" and so he suggested that a microteaching programme needed to incorporate three constituents - planning, performance and perception. Rules of planning were given in lectures and seminars and the student learned to split a topic into its component concepts, organise them into a suitable sequence and choose appropriate teaching methods. The performance aspect of teaching was analysed into component teaching skills which were demonstrated. Opportunities to practise these skills were given in microlessons with school pupils in order to improve performance. While the focus was mostly on the component skills some global practice was provided as a conclusion to microteaching to bring the skills together into an overall performance. Feedback was provided in the form of viewing and discussing videorecordings of the microlessons with a supervisor so that the students learned what cues to look for in their interactions with pupils. This perception of teacher-pupil interactions alerted the student to the effects of these teaching behaviours on his pupils, and these perceptions could then influence subsequent planning and performance. No reteach cycle was included, but students worked in teams of four and benefited from viewing and discussing all four lessons.

While Brown's work acknowledged and made use of Argyle's model of social skills training, this theoretical framework was much more strongly evident in the microteaching format developed by Hargie and coworkers and called 'Social Skills Training'. Hargie and Maidment (1979, Ch.7) have given a detailed account of this rationale for microteaching. Social Skills Training has been applied by Tittmar, Hargie and Dickson (1977) not only to train teachers but also other professionals, for example students in social work and health visiting, who need to use the skills of interpersonal behaviour and communication in situations such as counselling and interviewing. They have described their system of Social Skills Training as behavioural analysis and behaviour modification.

In applying Social Skills Training to teaching Hargie, Dickson and Tittmar (1978) have developed a microteaching format which they have called 'Mini-teaching' which they argue has overcome some of the disadvantages of the original Stanford Model. The component parts of the teaching act were broken down into separate skills, still virtually the same as in the Stanford Model - questioning, reinforcement, stimulus variation, explanation, illustration, set induction and closure. However a much more determined effort was made to apply the requirement of Argyle's Social Skills Training Model to integrate the skills back together again to reconstruct the whole teaching performance. Thus at certain stages in the programme sessions were devoted to integrating the skills covered so far in the course.

Another specific feature of mini-teaching was designed to bridge the gap between Social Skills Training and classroom teaching. The length of the lessons was increased gradually from 5 to 30 minutes and the number of pupils from 5 to 25. The final session involved the student teaching a full lesson to a full class, not in a microteaching laboratory but in a normal classroom setting, though still in the college environment. This lesson was still videotaped and the student was given both video and tutored feedback. Thus as a refinement of microteaching, mini-teaching fitted better into the theoretical framework of Argyle's Social Skills Training Model. Integrating the skills helped students appreciate that the skills interacted with one another and that they were to be regarded as techniques which the teacher could choose to utilise as deemed fit.

Hargie and Maidment (1978) also pointed to the importance of discrimination training as a component of microteaching. Discrimination training helped the trainee learn to identify the skill in action, to analyse critically its behavioural components and to evaluate its effectiveness. Discrimination training was provided through lectures relating the teaching skills to the theoretical framework derived from the social psychology of interpersonal behaviour and through videotaped models of the skill being demonstrated. Thus the trainee learned to identify the central features of the skill and to understand what was involved in using it, thereby coming to appreciate not only how to use the skill but when to use it.

In emphasising the importance of discrimination training Hargie and Maidment acknowledged that microteaching involved much more than practising the component skills of teaching and integrating them again. It played an important part in helping students develop an understanding of the teaching process. Indeed, all the approaches to

17

microteaching so far discussed have a strong academic component in which the identification and understanding of skills goes a long way to giving students a language to talk about teaching and helping them form their own views on teaching. Perhaps the practice of skills in microteaching is a means to an end and not an end in itself, and the permanent gains from microteaching are at the cognitive level rather than at the behavioural level of improved performance of skills? This idea that microteaching was not just about the modification of behaviours but concerned the modification of the cognitive structures of the learner was developed by McIntyre and coworkers.

The Cognitive Structures Approach

When microteaching was introduced at Stirling University the Component Skills Approach was used and the organisational format was mostly that used at Stanford. Immediately a programme of curriculum development and research work was initiated and was conducted over the period 1969-75. This research and development work has been reported by McIntyre, MacLeod and Griffiths (1977) and it led to the gradual development of an alternative rationale for microteaching.

The first change that was made was to replace the rating scales used to define each teaching skill and to provide the focus for discussion of the teaching performance in the feedback sessions. These scales were considered inadequate because of low reliability and because they emphasised evaluation of the teaching. McIntyre and coworkers wanted to focus on description and analysis of the teaching rather than on evaluation and so they developed and tested systematic observation instruments for each skill in order to describe the use of relevant aspects of teaching behaviour. For example, for the skill of 'Varying the Stimulus' the occurrence of the following classroom behaviours was recorded: teacher movement, teacher gesture, change in speech pattern, change in sensory focus, verbal participation and physical participation. A time sampling system was used and any of these six aspects which occurred within each thirty-second interval of the lesson was noted. The record showed the extent to which each behaviour was being utilised and it was by discussion of this record in relation to the particular lesson that the underlying reasons for use, or lack of use, of the skill was teased out between tutor and student.

18

Critical judgements as to the competence of the skill performance and its effectiveness could then follow.

Initially the component skills, derived from the Stanford Model, were used to focus attention on specific teaching behaviours and "to make explicit the criteria in terms of which students were asked to plan and evaluate these aspects of their teaching." However it was recognised that there was considerable doubt about the validity of these specified skills. The empirical research on classroom teaching, the relevant psychological theories and the consensus opinions of experienced teachers were interpreted as providing only appropriate suggestions and not authoritative statements.

> Given these circumstances one can only treat specified patterns of teaching behaviour as hypothetical skills of teaching. (McIntyre, MacLeod and Griffiths, 1977, p.33)

Thus the component skills were used at Stirling as an organisational feature of the programme rather than as a rationale.

One of the major goals at Stirling was to promote students' analytical reflection on their teaching and McIntyre and coworkers realised that, while there was already a substantial amount of research into microteaching, very little was actually known about the nature of student teachers' learning in microteaching. Accordingly, MacLeod set out to research the students' understanding of their own microteaching behaviour and its development.

Macleod (1976a) explored the meaning of students' microteaching behaviours not only in terms of the predetermined categories of the teacher trainers but also in terms of the students' own conceptual systems or schemata. He analysed students' written responses to their own microlessons after they received videotaped feedback. He found that as their microteaching experiences increased they showed an increasing trend towards evaluating their lesson in terms of those pupil behaviours prescribed as desirable. Their own teaching behaviours were evaluated in terms of how they were perceived to facilitate these desired pupil behaviours. MacLeod concluded that students' cognitive and perceptual structures were an important determinant of their teaching performance.

From this and other evidence from the researches at Stirling, MacLeod and McIntyre (1977) argued that the importance of the skills approach, and of skill-related feedback, was that it tended to produce changes in the students' cognitive repertoires through the incorporation of the skill concepts. It was this cognitive repertoire which then largely determined what students perceived of their performance, and it was these perceptions which largely determined subsequent performance and performance change. They posed a tentative cognitive model, formulated as a set of inferences drawn from their researches, as to how students learn in microteaching.

> Before entering microteaching programmes, each student has distinct, complex conceptual schemata relating to teaching and these schemata have strong evaluative associations.

> There are large individual differences in these conceptual schemata, but large areas of commonality may also exist through the embedding of these schemata within the ideologies of teaching subjects.

> These conceptual schemata show a high degree of stability, but gradual change can occur through the acquisition of new constructs and principles from instruction and experience.

> Students' conceptual schemata to a large extent control their teaching behaviour, and changes in teaching behaviour result from changes in schemata. (p.117)

These inferences provided a cognitive interpretation of microteaching which could be regarded as a means of producing changes in the students' cognitive structures about teaching, helping them develop their own self-concept as teacher.

Griffiths (1977) considered the implications of this cognitive model in relation to the role that skill definition, modelling and feedback played in the microteaching process. He argued that, rather than being defined by descriptions of observable teaching behaviours, the skills should be defined in terms of "manageable concepts which teachers can use in processing the information which arises from the complexity of classroom interaction." This

framework of concepts could then be applied by
teachers in order to make decisions about when to
use the skill and also to help them be perceptive of
the skill-in-action so that a valid evaluation of
skill performance could be made. Modelling the
skills would help the students incorporate the skill
concepts into their cognitive structures. The
feedback component of microteaching would provide
information which the student could relate to his
existing conceptual schemata of teaching, thereby
refining and extending this conceptualisation.
MacLeod and McIntyre saw this conceptual development
through self-evaluation as being the main thrust of
microteaching which provided both instruction and
experiences for "the development and induction of
functional and adaptive cognitive structures."

This section has summarised the different
approaches to microteaching up to the time of our
own researches. We shall return, in the last
chapter, to a further discussion of the various
rationales for microteaching in the light of our own
findings. Before reporting our research we need to
give a more detailed account of how microteaching
was operating at the New University of Ulster during
the period of our investigations.

MICROTEACHING AT THE NEW UNIVERSITY OF ULSTER

We have already outlined the rationale underpinning
Brown's development of microteaching at this
institution. The social psychological emphasis on
teaching as social interaction, together with the
notion of teaching as an intentional activity
providing learning gains for pupils, were used to
focus on the planning, performance and perception
aspects of learning to teach. The organisational
arrangements were improved as this new institution
expanded and the numbers of students taking
microteaching each week grew rapidly to about 200.
The details of the programme were also modified
gradually on the basis of experiences, research
studies (Brown, 1973, 1975d) and discussions with
tutors, students, school teachers and pupils.
Examples of the early changes that were made were
the dropping of the reteach sessions and the
introduction of new rating scales for the teaching
skills.
Research showed that the 'scores' obtained for
the reteach sessions using the rating scales were

almost always lower than the equivalent 'scores' for the teach sessions. Also, students expressed dislike of the reteach sessions. There were several possible reasons for these findings. Firstly, since viewing and discussing the teach microlesson gave both students and tutors a learning experience, the aims of the two sessions were different. In the teach session the aims were to provide a learning gain for pupils and to practise a teaching skill, whereas the aims of the reteach session were to improve the lesson through changes in the lesson plan and in the performance of those teaching skills identified in the critique session as significant factors influencing the learning outcomes. Consequently the one teaching skill rating scale need not necessarily be relevant in both situations and, even if it was, the focus of analysis and evaluation was different on the two occasions so the teach and reteach scores on the rating scale should not be compared and interpreted as indicating an improvement or deterioration in performance. A second reason was that the planned weekly cycle of events (plan - teach - critique - replan - reteach - critique) was not actually put fully into operation. The organisational arrangements did not provide students with an adequate opportunity to replan the lesson, so it was not surprising that students felt they were doing worse in the reteach sessions.

The possibility of improving the contribution of the reteach was not followed up and the reteach was dropped from the system. This decision was probably more a matter of expediency than the result of research findings because the growth rate in student numbers at this time far exceeded the rate of appointment of new staff so that the system was under considerable strain in coping with the through-put of students each week. Removing the reteach and having students work in groups of four with one tutor alleviated this problem.

Another early development was to modify the Stanford rating scales for the separate teaching skills and develop new ones of tested reliability and validity. Also, a new global rating scale, the Lesson Appraisal Guide, was introduced to give a measure of overall teaching performance. This used a 7-point rating scale to judge the fourteen different aspects of the teaching performance listed in Figure 1.3.

Staff views were also a formative influence on the programme development. In particular the tutors of English and other humanities and creative arts

Fig. 1.3: Lesson Appraisal Guide

1. Gaining pupils' attention
2. Explanation and narration
3. Giving directions
4. Asking and adapting questions
5. Recognising difficulties of understanding
6. Voice and speech habits
7. Non-verbal cues
8. Encouraging appropriate responses
9. Holding pupils' attention
10. Gaining pupil participation
11. Pupil control
12. Use of aids
13. Allocation of time for pupil learning
14. Lesson planning and structure

subjects wanted to strengthen the interaction of
subject content, pupils' learning and teaching
skills and they doubted the validity of practising
specific skills out of context. They argued that
students learning to teach these subjects had to
take their essential nature into account and that
the creation of attitudes and feelings, as well as
gains in language skills, needed to be reflected in
students' experiences of learning to teach these
subjects. A number of changes were made to take
these points into account. The tutors could
increase their support of students in lesson
planning and discussion in order to take advantage
of those features of microteaching which were
considered valuable to particular teaching subjects.
A more flexible use of teaching time was permitted.
The students could choose to plan as a team so that
one student could start the lesson theme, another
develop it and another teach the concluding section.
Alternatively, instead of teaching a short lesson
every week, the student could on occasions teach a
double length lesson. After these early
modifications the microteaching system settled into
an ongoing steady state that is still in operation.

The system in operation

The practical teaching studies programme is a
compulsory part of the teacher education courses
which are four year programmes in which the academic
subject and education are studied concurrently.
Successful students obtain an honours degree in
their academic subject inclusive of a teaching
qualification. The practical studies programme

23

consists of school visits in the first year for classroom observation studies, university-based microteaching in the second year and block teaching practice in schools in the third year. The microteaching programme lasts for twelve weeks and contains two parallel components, the weekly lectures and the practical component incorporating teach and review sessions.

The weekly lectures are given by the course organiser and include instruction in lesson planning and in teaching skill recognition. The students are presented at the lecture with a microteaching exercise, normally focused on one particular skill, to be prepared for the next week's teach session. Brown's book (1975b), "Microteaching, a programme of teaching skills", is used as the course text to help students plan these exercises. The lectures also cover the research evidence on teaching, teacher education, microteaching and the teaching skills. Other aspects of teaching are also considered, such as discipline and classroom management, organisation of classroom space, teacher expectations, mixed ability teaching, provision for individualised learning, etc., so that a comprehensive overview of teaching in presented.

The teach and review sessions take place under the supervision of an experienced tutor who is free to adopt his own approach. During the first week of lectures the year group of up to 200 students is organised into groups of four, usually according to their curriculum interests, and they familiarise themselves with the layout of the microclassroom and learn to use the recording equipment in the control room. Where possible tutors with similar curriculum backgrounds are assigned to them. The large number of students usually means that all education tutors are involved as supervisors.

When microteaching practice begins each group is allocated to a one hour teaching session and the usual format is that each student teaches a fifteen minute lesson each week to a class of six to eight ten-year old pupils. The teaching is real and the pupils are genuine learners collected on a once a week basis from nine local primary schools. Figure 1.4 shows the organisation of the programme.

The microteaching practice takes place in a suite of five microclassrooms with associated control rooms and viewing rooms that have facilities for videotape playback and review. The suite also contains a large reception room for the visiting classes, and an administrative office. Each

Fig. 1.4: The N.U.U. microteaching programme

Wk.	Lecture	Practice Session	
1.	Microteaching	Group organisation	
2.	Teaching a concept	Equipment operation	
3.	Lesson planning	Teaching peers	
4.	Set and closure	Teaching pupils	
5.	Teacher explanation	Teaching pupils	
6.	Teacher liveliness	Teaching pupils	
7.	Pupil reinforcement	Teaching pupils	
8.	Pupil participation	Teaching pupils	
9.	Fluency in questioning	Teaching pupils	
10.	Higher order questions	Teaching pupils	
11.	Integrating the skills	Teaching pupils	*
12.	Teacher/pupil interaction, environmental factors	Teaching pupils	*

* Last two lessons assessed on global skills

microclassroom is specially prepared in terms of carpeting and lighting to facilitate recording and has two cameras mounted unobtrusively near the ceiling at the back and front of the room. The cameras have wide angled lenses providing fixed fields of view of the blackboard and teaching space at the front and of the pupils' workplaces. Before the lessons begin the students can arrange the furniture to facilitate their teaching and set the camera angles to ensure the cameras can view both teacher and pupils at work. In the adjacent control room, monitoring enables the view from either camera to be selected for videorecording so that teacher-pupil interactions can be followed. Split screen effects can be employed if required.

Production of the one hour videotape is left entirely to the group of students. While one teaches, the others observe the lesson in the control room and operate the equipment. No technical support is required to produce the videotape. The operation of the equipment is checked quickly at the start of each week and occasional equipment breakdowns are handled by a technician providing stand-by equipment and taking the faulty equipment away for repair to the university's television studio. Thus the system operates with the most basic of equipment and the minimum of technical assistance. An ancillary staff member conducts the pupils to and from the microteaching suite by bus and ensures the students

25

are keeping to their time schedule.

After the teaching session the group view the videotape of the lessons with their tutor at an agreed convenient time. This review session may take up to two hours. Microteaching tutors have developed their own approach to microteaching from the experiences of previous years. The high degree of flexibility open to the individual tutor and their group is indicated by the differing ways in which the system is employed. Some supervisors are known to attend the live teaching sessions to help plan their approach to the review sessions, while others deliberately stay away so that the students' expressed needs are used to focus the review sessions. A number of tutors prefer holding the review conference on the same day as the teaching session while others leave it until a few days later. Certain tutors encourage their students to teach thirty-minute lessons occasionally in which case not all of their students would be teaching each week, whereas others prefer their students to teach every week. While some supervisors appear sympathetic to the content of the lecture programme, others are thought to ignore the lecture programme completely.

One extremely important feature of the system is that it is assessed and the tutor plays a large part in the assessment, so students view their tutor as examiner as well as adviser and counsellor. The assessment is based on 70% for the practical component and 30% for a written examination. The examination tests the understanding of teaching, teacher education, microteaching and teaching skills as presented in the lecture programme and the supporting reading references.

The crucial aspect for students is that they must pass the practical component of the assessment in order to proceed with a course incorporating a teaching qualification. Those that fail are required to transfer into a degree programme in an academic subject. This is a major influence on students' approaches to their microteaching and to their relationships with their tutor. Tutors too find assessment a major influence on their work. Some try to separate their roles as adviser and examiner by using the last two lessons for assessment only, so that there are no review conferences with students in those weeks. Others continue the review conferences right to the end of the programme feeling able to integrate their examining and tutorial roles. Thus, while the

programme has an underlying rationale in terms of
its design, students' experiences of its operation
depend very much on whom they have as their tutor
and on the working relationships that develop
between them.

We were interested in describing what was
happening to students during their microteaching in
terms of their experiences and learning gains. We
wanted to understand the processes operating in
microteaching and identify the underlying
pedagogical constructs in order to tease out how
microteaching was contributing to the process of
learning to teach. Our preliminary investigations
are described in the next chapter and we show how
they led us on to more focused research studies.

Chapter 2.

EXPLORATORY INVESTIGATIONS

It has already been suggested that there was a need
for descriptive studies into students' learning in
microteaching and for more research instruments to
collect information about microteaching. For these
reasons, and also to take account of some of the
unique features of the microteaching system at the
New University of Ulster, a number of exploratory
investigations were undertaken. The intention was
to provide a basis of description upon which to
build more definitive research studies. This
chapter outlines these exploratory studies which
involved observational studies of the microlessons
and review conferences and the development of
methods of investigating the relationships between
the supervising tutor and his students and the
contribution that microteaching was making to
students' growth into teachers. Finally, we show
how these studies indicated promising aspects of
microteaching for further research.

AN OBSERVATION STUDY OF MICROLESSONS

This exploratory study, undertaken by McGarvey and
Harris in 1975, investigated the nature of the
microlessons that students were teaching. It was
conducted with two aims in mind. Firstly, a
description of students' microlessons should
contribute to an understanding of students'
experiences of microteaching and hence to finding
out what students were learning in microteaching.
Secondly, viewing microlessons gave an opportunity
to apply the Lesson Appraisal Guide (LAG), the
rating schedule for global teaching skills developed
by Brown (see Figure 1.3). The objective of this
try-out of the LAG was to see if the scores that it

28

produced could be used with confidence as valid research measures.

Videotapes of the microlessons of 120 students in each of weeks 6 and 9 of the programme were viewed and rated using the LAG by McGarvey and Harris working independently. The videotapes were given a secret identity code and mixed randomly so that the researchers, both experienced microteaching tutors, could not tell whether a particular videotape was a week 6 or week 9 recording. The researchers first talked over the meaning of each item of the rating scale so that an agreed definition of each item was being used, but no training in the application of the LAG was undertaken. This was deliberate because training in the use of LAG would have necessitated the researchers reaching agreement about their interpretations of teaching and about their evaluations of the quality of teaching skills. For purposes of checking the consistency with which the researchers were able to apply LAG, three microlessons were selected at random from the batch of 240 microlessons already viewed and were rated a second time. During the viewing the researchers also kept note of their subjective impressions and afterwards wrote short accounts of their overall impressions of the microlessons.

Item analysis of the results obtained confirmed Brown's finding that the LAG was a homogeneous rating scale of high internal consistency, Cronbach's alpha coefficient for the two judges being 0.91 and 0.90. Also, both researchers were found to be applying the rating scale reasonably consistently as a comparison of the results for the three lessons which were viewed twice gave correlation coefficients of 0.80 and 0.67 as indications of intra-observer agreement. However, tests of inter-observer agreement for use of the individual items of LAG showed almost zero correlation ($r=0.06$). The judges were differing markedly in their application of the LAG and calculation of a reliability coefficient as an intraclass correlation coefficient by applying a two way analysis of variance (Shrout and Fleiss, 1979) to the total LAG scores for the repeat viewings of the three videotapes (3 lessons by 2 observers with 2 repeat ratings) gave $r = -0.24$. Examination of the analysis of variance data showed that the low reliability was mainly due to a very big interaction effect with the bias of judges changing markedly across the three microlessons.

Since the judges were consistent, but
different, this raised problems about the validity
of the LAG as a research instrument. There were
quite a number of possible reasons for the disparity
of the researchers' opinions. For example, they may
have been applying different value systems about
teaching, they may have had different perceptions of
the teaching behaviours, or they may have had
different conceptualisations of the loosely
described behaviours. In order to apply the LAG as
a research instrument it would have been necessary
to be more explicit about the theoretical view of
teaching that was being promoted, to define the
teaching behaviours more precisely and to reach a
concensus view among tutors as to the values about
teaching which were to be applied. This the
researchers were not prepared to do because
discussions with tutors at the New University of
Ulster, and the views of tutors expressed in
McIntyre, MacLeod and Griffith's book (1977),
suggested that tutors held very different views
about microteaching. The researchers did not want
to begin a research programme by constraining at the
outset an issue which could turn out to be an
important source of variability. Thus they decided
against using a rating schedule for global teaching
skills for research purposes because the question of
"Whose ratings?" was likely to be an important
constituent of the investigations.

Since both judges had applied LAG consistently,
the unscrambling of the randomised microlessons
allowed a comparison of the students' performances
in weeks 6 and 9 of the programme. The judges both
found that there was no change in the mean LAG score
obtained for the whole year group. Even this
finding could not be stated with confidence because
a global teaching skills rating schedule was being
applied in circumstances in which students were
being asked to teach lessons which afforded
opportunities to practice specific teaching skills.

The other purpose of this investigation had
been to describe the nature of the microlessons and
collect the researchers' subjective impressions
about students' learning in microteaching.
Interestingly, the vast literature of research into
microteaching does not appear to contain a single
article which describes students at work in their
microlessons, though a considerable number of
articles do discuss tutors' reservations about what
students are being asked to do and can achieve. The
experience of watching 240 microlessons was a very

enlightening one for the researchers giving much
food for thought and challenging many assumptions
about what students were accomplishing in their
microlessons. Viewing the microlessons of all
students revealed the challenges of microteaching
much more starkly than did the usual tutor's role of
working with a small number of students throughout
the programme.

The first overall impression was one of
pleasure at the high level of professional
responsibility that students were applying to their
work and the second was a realisation of the
enormity of the task that they had been set and were
struggling diligently to achieve. The students were
undoubtedly having very valuable experiences in
microteaching and were learning much more about
teaching and about themselves as teachers than was
being assumed in a component skills rationale for
microteaching. As well as practising teaching
skills they were finding out about pupils'
behaviour, personalities, capabilities, interests
and thoughts. They were exploring their own
relationships with children and finding the level of
language needed to hold conversations with pupils.
They were learning about management problems and the
control of the learning process - what does the
student do in a microlesson when a pupil launches
into a long anecdotal account which is obviously
important to the pupil but is of little relevance to
the student's task of practising a specific teaching
skill within a restricted time allocation?

The researchers quickly found that teaching a
microlesson was a very complex task - just as
complicated as teaching an ordinary lesson in a
classroom, but different. The idea that
microteaching presented students with a simplified
teaching situation was no longer tenable to the
researchers. Moreover, microteaching was presenting
students with its own unique set of difficulties.
The students did not know their pupils well. They
knew nothing about their background knowledge and
levels of ability and hence they found it very
difficult to select teaching topics which were
neither too easy nor too difficult. Also, pupils'
behaviour was often not typical of that in normal
classroom situations. The small group situation
seemed to magnify the influence of the behaviour of
individuals. This could be the very able pupil who
could anticipate the flow of the lesson and provide
answers before the questions were posed, or the
restless pupil who treated the situation as an

outing from school. Other pupils reacted very timidly to this different environment and school-teachers, who had accompanied their pupils to the university and had watched the live lessons on the control room monitor, sometimes commented on the almost unrecognisable behaviour of their pupils.

It was also apparent that the time scale of the microlesson imposed its own rhythm on the teaching. Many students reacted to this by assuming that there was not sufficient time for pupil activity and so a common approach was to develop the lesson through teacher's questions and pupils' verbal answers. Activity was reduced as acceptable learning behaviour and talk was emphasised. This was particularly noticeable for humanities students and less so for science and mathematics students, only a few of whom did avoid handling materials and making measurements.

Watching the microlessons emphasised to the researchers the difficulties that students were experiencing in coping with the tension between curriculum content and teaching skills. The programme was supposed to be about teaching skills, yet the students had to teach something, with the intention that pupils would learn. There were many examples of lessons in which the students appeared to be more concerned with organising the content within their own heads than in engaging the pupils as learners. There were other cases where students practised social skills and created 'good' teacher-pupil interactions, but these social skills never became teaching skills because no learning actually took place. These impressions led Joe Harris to describe the pupils' role in microteaching as "fodder for the teaching grind, rather than learners and developers of their own skills." This comment pointed to a weakness in many of the early rationales for microteaching - an emphasis on teacher performance can undervalue the purpose of teaching which is to facilitate learning. A cosy chat with some pupils in which the student displays good social skills is a much less threatening challenge for the student than that of ensuring that the interaction does actually produce some learning gains.

There was also food for thought in the microlessons to question assumptions about the universal application of teaching skills. There were quite clear differences in the teaching style of students teaching different curriculum subjects. These differences were evident in both the range of skills employed and the way in which they were being used. Microteaching seemed very well suited to helping science students develop organisational skills for practical work, whereas the needs of humanities students to engage pupils in affective learning seemed constrained. The way in which higher order questioning was being used in the humanities appeared to be different from its use in science.

There was some evidence in the videorecordings of some constraint being imposed on students by the physical environment of the teaching laboratory. The limitations of static fields of view of the cameras, slight as these limitations were, imposed on some students an imagined restriction in the use of space. Such students felt obliged to perform 'on stage' and imposed on themselves disadvantages in such activities as using visual aids and allowing pupil movement.

It was an assumption in this format of microteaching that the other students in the group were watching the live lesson on the monitor in the control room. One task that the watching students had to do was to control which camera view was being recorded by simply pressing one or other button on a switching device. It was possible to use the equipment to record action around the room and capture interactive sequences like: teacher questions - pupils react - one pupil answers - teacher responds. It was also possible to record the teacher's travels as she moved around interacting with individual pupils working at their places. This role of vidoetape producer was sometimes neglected by the student observers and the resultant recordings did not realise the full potential of the equipment. Long periods of watching a blank blackboard while the sound recording was indicating that the teacher was down among the children doing interesting things left the researchers wondering what the other students were doing at this time and how they were forming views about the live lesson to feed into the later review session.

The message from this viewing of microlessons was that the planning of a short microlesson is a highly specialised skill if it is framed in terms of practising a specific skill and ensuring that the pupils make learning gains. This latter objective means that organising the lesson content and materials and using other teaching skills must also be considered. Planning and teaching a very short

lesson to meet both these objectives was simply
beyond the ability of these inexperienced student
teachers who did not have the opportunity to know
their pupils well. The skills under focus in the
two weeks in which the microlessons were observed
were teacher explanation and higher order
questioning. The researchers were not able to tell
from the randomised lessons which skill was being
practised. Indeed, the limitations imposed on many
students by inadequate lesson planning and their
concern about content development meant that they
were not able to concentrate on the practice of
isolated skills at all.

Despite some of these impressions the
researchers were more convinced than ever that
microteaching was a valuable component of teacher
education. It was the assumptions underlying the
rationale for microteaching which were at fault and
not the system itself. In particular, the
assumptions about what teaching a microlesson
actually involved and about the tasks which
inexperienced students could accomplish were
limiting the students' learning potential
unnecessarily. The researchers formed the following
opinions from their viewing of the videotapes.

Inexperienced students working with pupils whom
they do not know are not able to plan and
execute microlessons which allow them to focus
on a specific teaching skill.

Teaching a short microlesson to a small group
is different from teaching an ordinary lesson
to a class. It is different in aims,
structure, pace, rhythm, pupil activity and
pupils' response patterns. It has already been
said that it is not simplified teaching - the
researchers would add that it is also not
simulated classroom teaching. It is real
teaching of a different type and is just as
complex as classroom teaching.

Concentrating on those teaching skills that are
generalisable across the curriculum is too
restrictive an approach. This tends to
emphasise the social role of these skills at
the expense of their teaching role. There is a
need to place the skills in their curriculum
context so that their effectiveness can be
considered in terms of pupil learning rather
than just by rating the quality of the skill

performance.

Microteaching presents students with much more
varied opportunities for learning than is
allowed for in a component skills approach to
teaching. Teaching microlessons incorporates
other aspects of teaching. As well as trying
out their performance skills students are using
the opportunity to:
  find out about children;
  explore their own relationships with
  children;
  explore their feelings and attitudes about
  the role of teacher;
  learn to select those teaching skills
  relevant to the context;
  make decisions about what to do next in
  response to the pupils' initiatives.

With hindsight it is not surprising that the
researchers did not find the Lesson Appraisal Guide
a helpful general research instrument. Not only did
its structure assume that any lesson is scorable
within LAG's theoretical context, but it implied
that all of its listed skills were to be observed in
any lesson and that no other skills were important.
The basis of using LAG as a research instrument
would be to compare the scores of different students
or the scores of one student on different occasions.
This would clearly be problematic because of the
difficulties that students were experiencing in
handling the tension between content and skills.
    The initial purpose in viewing the microlessons
was to produce a background of descriptive
information on which to base a major research
investigation, possibly a comparative study of some
of the components of microteaching. Rather than
proceed to investigations which would test
hypotheses drawn from an accepted theoretical
viewpoint, the research questions that had emerged
were concerned with the assumptions about students'
learning in microteaching and about the constructs
underpining the processes of microteaching.

OBSERVING MICROTEACHING REVIEW CONFERENCES

Providing feedback to students about their teaching
is a very important part of the microteaching cycle.
In the New University of Ulster the students obtain
this feedback at review conferences, at which the

supervising tutor and the group of four students view and discuss the videorecordings of each student's microlesson. In this way the student not only obtains feedback about his own lesson and teaching skills, but also has the opportunity to learn by viewing and discussing the other lessons. The way in which these conferences operate is a matter for each group to decide. The tutor is the only experienced member of the group and is also responsible for the final assessment of the students so it is to be expected that the tutor plays a dominant role in the review conference. Tutors have not received any training as microteaching supervisors and have developed their own approach through experience. Thus it was considered fruitful to investigate the various ways in which tutors were interpreting their role as supervisors, and how the review conference was contributing to the learning that students were gaining from microteaching.

The early research evidence about the effectiveness of supervision in microteaching was conflicting. Waimon and Ramseyer (1970) and Young and coworkers (1971) had failed to find any significant differences between supervised and unsupervised microteaching with regard to effectiveness. The main argument advanced for the development of the Minicourses as self-instructional inservice courses which did not require supervisors was that the research evidence was taken to suggest that the presence of a supervisor made little or no difference to experienced teachers in terms of behavioural gains (Perrott, 1972). However other studies, e.g. Berliner (1969), McDonald and Allen (1967), had noted significant gains from supervisory feedback. In reviewing the research into the supervision of microteaching, Griffiths (1972) concluded that "efforts to justify either supervisor or no supervisor involvement in microteaching programmes must be premature." None of the early research studies included a full account of the supervisory process to indicate exactly what the supervision entailed, so a description of microteaching supervision at the New University of Ulster should help identify some of the ways in which microteaching supervision can be conducted. We shall return to a more detailed discussion of the literature on supervision in Chapter Three.

In order to study the contribution that the review conferences were making to the microteaching process and the nature of the supervision that the students were experiencing, a systematic observation analysis system was developed. It was decided to use a systematic observation approach rather than an ethnographic approach because of the possibilities that systematic observation gave of researching a fairly large number of cases and of providing descriptive data which could be used for comparative purposes over a number of years of investigation. The processes whereby the Microteaching Review Conference Interaction Analysis System (MRCIAS) was created have been reported (Brown and McGarvey, 1975). MRCIAS was developed as a category system, in order to describe the sequential pattern of verbal interaction, rather than as a sign system, which would only count the number of different types of behaviour which occurred in a specified time interval without regard to their sequence.

The system was applied to videorecordings of review conferences so that two dimensions of conference talk could be coded by repeated viewing. The first dimension coded the discussions in terms of the issues being discussed. The trials identified the categories of subject content being utilised. The occurrence of each category of subject content was recorded as a percentage of the total talk. The coding of categories was applied at the end of every thought unit, which was regarded as the smallest section of verbal behaviour which conveyed a single thought.

The second analysis coded the pattern of verbal interaction among the participants and also the substantive meaning of the conference as a problem solving exercise. This dimension concentrated on the tutor's role since the developmental trials indicated that this was a major influence on conference discussions. The assumption that problem solving was an important task in supervision was derived from the studies of Blumberg (1970) who investigated the supervisor-teacher interactions in dyadic supervisory conferences. This viewpoint regarded the supervisory process to be aimed at improving the student teacher's skills through collaborative discussions in which the student teacher saw the supervisor as a source of help in identifying and analysing difficulties, providing relevant information about teaching and suggesting ways by which improvement could be achieved.

The MRCIAS codings of verbal behaviours were presented as a matrix of two-step chains of interaction using Flander's technique (1970). A set of interaction indices characteristic of the interaction pattern was then derived from the

37

matrix. Figure 2.1 summarises the MRCIAS categories and the problem solving and interaction indices derived from the matrix analysis. Appendix A describes the categories in more detail and explains the matrix analysis and the indices derived from it.

In order to accept that this observation system was a worthwhile research instrument it was necessary to demonstrate that it could yield reliable data and that its application to a review conference would reveal interesting descriptive features which could be taken as characteristic of that particular conference, distinguishing it from other conferences. Two observers were trained to use the observation system until a satisfactory level of inter-observer agreement with the researcher was reached. The criterion set for acceptable inter-observer agreement was that the Pi coefficients (Scott, 1955), comparing the observers' distributions of total thought units across the categories, should not be less than 0.85.

A reliability trial was then conducted in which the observers and researcher separately coded three review conference discussions. Since the content dimension was summarised as the percentage distribution of conference talk across the content categories, the Scott Pi coefficient was taken as an acceptable indicator of reliability. Values of Pi calculated for the content categories of MRCIAS were all satisfactory. The problem solving and interaction indices were taken as the observational measures for purposes of calculating reliability for the interactive dimension. Reliability coefficients for these measures were calculated by one-way analysis of variance as recommended by Rowley (1976) and Medley and Mitzel (1963). The values obtained were in the range 0.7 - 1.0 and were considered acceptable.

Videorecordings were made of 24 review groups, 18 of which were recorded on two different occasions and the other 6 on three occasions giving 54 recordings in all. The recording of more than one conference for each group would allow the stability of conference behaviours to be investigated from occasion to occasion. The 24 review groups involved 18 different tutors, 6 of whom were supervising two groups. This sample of tutors was deliberately selected to give a wide range of tutor types and was composed of 11 university lecturers (3 from educational studies and 8 from curriculum studies), and 7 post-graduate students taking the taught M.A. in Education course (3 who had just completed their

Fig. 2.1: The Microteaching Review Conference
Interaction Analysis System   (MRCIAS)

CONTENT DIMENSION
   1.   Structuring
   2.   Teaching skill under focus
   3.   Other teaching skills and behaviours
   4.   Lesson organisation and structure
   5.   Lesson subject content
   6.   Lesson materials and aids
   7.   Pupils' characteristics and behaviours
   8.   Discipline and control
   9.   Preparations for next week's lesson
   10. Preparations for next week's skills
   11. The microteaching system
   12. Other talk
   13. Silence
   14. Non-codable talk

PROBLEM SOLVING AND VERBAL INTERACTION DIMENSION
   1.   Tutor gives information
   2.   Tutor gives analysis
   3.   Tutor gives suggestion
   4.   Tutor asks for information
   5.   Tutor asks for analysis
   6.   Tutor asks for suggestion
   7.   Tutor accepts, responds
   8.   Tutor other talk
   9.   Student No. 1 talks
   10. Student No. 2 talks
   11. Student No. 3 talks
   12. Student No. 4 talks
   13. Silence
   14. Non-codable talk

PROBLEM SOLVING AND INTERACTION INDICES
   1.   Tutor/student talk ratio
   2.   Tutor information ratio
   3.   Tutor analysis ratio
   4.   Tutor suggestion ratio
   5.   Tutor extended talk ratio
   6.   Tutor questioning ratio
   7.   Tutor response ratio
   8.   Tutor acceptance/response ratio
   9.   Tutor indirect/direct ratio
   10. Student interaction ratio
   11. Student initiation/response ratio
   12. Student extended talk ratio

undergraduate degree and 4 experienced
schoolteachers on secondment). The inclusion in the
sample of 6 tutors who were each supervising two
groups gave the opportunity to study the stability
of the supervisor's influence on the conference
interactions. The student teachers were drawn from
the complete range of curriculum specialisms. The
observers worked separately each coding different
batches of the 54 review conference videotapes.
Some aspects of the data obtained are now discussed
to illustrate the ways in which the review
conferences can be described and indicate the
potential of this approach for researching students'
experiences of microteaching.

The variety of approaches to microteaching review

Striking differences were found among the review
groups in the content of discussion, the style of
interaction and the focus on problem solving. The
following examples illustrate these differences.
Table 2.1 shows the distribution of conference talk
across MRCIAS content categories for three review
conferences.

Group A concentrated on global teaching skills
(58%) with no attention given to the teaching skill
which was supposed to be practised in the lesson.
The lesson plan and structure (17%) figured
prominently in their discussions and the behaviour
of the pupils (9%) was also considered in some
detail. Group B not only ignored the 'skill of the
week' but gave relatively little attention to global
skills (18%), talking mostly about the lesson (38%),
covering its structure (21%) and plans for next
weeks' lesson (14%). This group also talked about
the pupils (22%) and discipline (11%) in what was
overall a wide ranging discussion. Group C
conformed much more closely to the expected pattern
of discussion, talking 26% of thought units about
the skill under focus, 14% about other skills and
14% about planning for future use of skills. Even
here discussing the lesson still accounted for 20%
of talk so discussing the skills required also the
discussion of the context in which the skills were
being performed.

The problem solving and interaction
characteristics of review conferences were
summarised by the indices derived from the MRCIAS
interaction matrix. Table 2.2 shows the indices
obtained from three example conferences. Using the
indices to compare these examples with the composite
picture from all 54 conferences and referring to the

interaction matrices to elicit points of detail
yielded the following descriptions of these
conferences.

Table 2.1: The content of example review discussions

MRCIAS Content Dimension Categories	% use by		
	Gp.A	Gp.B	Gp.C
1. Structuring	3.8	2.6	2.6
2. Teaching skill under focus	0.5	0.0	25.5
3. Other teaching skills	58.1	17.9	14.0
4. Lesson structure	16.6	21.4	20.3
5. Lesson subject content	0.0	2.2	7.4
6. Lesson materials and aids	0.0	0.0	1.5
7. Pupils' behaviours	9.1	22.3	3.3
8. Discipline and control	3.0	11.4	0.0
9. Next week's lesson	0.0	14.4	5.2
10. Next week's skills	0.0	0.0	14.0
11. The microteaching system	2.8	1.3	1.1
12. Other talk	0.0	3.9	1.9
13. Silence	5.9	2.2	3.0
14. Non-codable talk	0.2	0.4	0.4

Table 2.2: Problem solving and interaction indices
for example review conference discussions

Problem solving and interaction indices	Review groups		
	X	Y	Z
1. Tutor/student talk	1.93	1.76	4.78
2. Tutor information	0.50	0.49	0.84
3. Tutor analysis	0.15	0.27	0.03
4. Tutor suggestion	0.08	0.02	0.02
5. Tutor extended talk	0.57	0.66	0.70
6. Tutor questioning	0.16	0.09	0.16
7. Tutor response	0.26	0.19	0.10
8. Tutor acceptance/response	0.67	0.74	0.58
9. Tutor indirect/direct	0.74	0.43	0.35
10. Student interaction	0.04	0.02	0.01
11. Student initiation/response	0.29	0.60	0.96
12. Student extended talk	0.45	0.64	0.39

<u>Conference X</u> This tutor was appreciably more indirect in style than average and there was more than average tutor questioning. This tutor's questioning style was successful in gaining student participation and the use of silence as 'wait time' and the support and encouragement given to student responses were contributory factors. Even so the group was strongly tutor dominated with very few student-student interactions and a low level of student initiation of conversation. There was less than average information level discussion and more than average suggestions made to help the students, so there was a problem solving perspective to the discussions.

<u>Conference Y</u> This conference had a strong analytical focus. Most of the analysis was given by the tutor rather than being drawn from the students by questioning, suggesting a fairly critical approach by the tutor. The tutor did respond to student talk with more than average acceptance behaviour. There was virtually no student-student interaction, all talk being to and from the tutor. A noticeable pattern was 'tutor telling' followed by silence followed by more 'tutor telling'. There were few suggestions for improvement.

<u>Conference Z</u> This tutor used the examples taken from the videotape viewing as points of departure for long accounts, at the information providing level, of his own views on teaching. He did ask a reasonable number of questions, but these were mostly asking for information about the lesson structure. Students did interject some comments into the flow of tutor talk, but these were of short duration and were not taken up and reinforced by the tutor, who continued with more information providing talk. There was no student-student interaction and almost no problem solving activity analysing the lesson and teaching skills and suggesting improvements.

These examples illustrate how individual review conferences can be described. How characteristic are these behaviours of the group? Are the groups distinguishable one from another by their behaviours? Do a group's behaviour patterns remain relatively stable from conference to conference? Do different groups who have the same tutor have similar problem solving and interactive behaviours? The sample of groups and conferences that was videorecorded allowed some preliminary exploration of these questions, with the twelve MRCIAS problem solving and interaction indices providing the descriptive variables for investigation.

Thirteen groups each having a different tutor and each of which was observed on two occasions were compared by a one way analysis of variance. Was the variation between the groups more marked than the variation within the groups from occasion to occasion? Ten out of the twelve problem solving and interaction indices gave significant F values ($p < 0.05$). Another comparison was made of six tutors, each of whom was supervising two groups. These twelve groups had each been recorded on two separate occasions. This gave a completely nested one dimensional analysis of variance design (Dayton, 1970, p.209) with occasions nested within groups and tutors, and groups nested within tutors. The twelve problem solving and interaction indices again provided the conference variables. Ten out of the twelve indices were found to give significant F values ($p < 0.05$). For seven out of these ten indices there was a significant effect for groups and for three indices there was a significant effect for tutors. The groups were showing reasonably stable and characteristic patterns of behaviour from occasion to occasion and groups that had the same tutor had some similar features.

Thus the problem solving and interaction indices looked promising as reliable measures of review conference behaviours, reliability here being interpreted in the sense that differences obtained between measures of the same group on different occasions are small compared to the differences between measures obtained for different groups (Medley and Mitzel, 1963).

Outcomes
This exploratory study had been concerned with developing a systematic observation instrument, MRCIAS, for microteaching review conferences and with investigating its potential for research by applying it to study a sample of review conference discussions selected to encompass a wide range of conference variables. It had been demonstrated that observers could be trained to use the system at a satisfactory level of inter-observer agreement. The system was designed to concentrate on the behaviours of the supervising tutor, a decision which was justified in view of the very dominant, directing role that most tutors played in the conferences. It

had been found to yield reliable data in the sense
that characteristic features of conference
discussions could be identified and used to
distinguish the review groups one from another.
Groups differed in the subject content of their
discussions, in their use of a problem solving
approach and in their patterns of interaction.

Because of the selective nature of the sample
these exploratory findings could not be stated with
any confidence. What could be said at this stage
was that MRCIAS did have potential as a research
instrument. It could yield reliable data which
would reveal interesting insights and which could be
used to characterise conference behaviours and
distinguish different approaches to the supervision
of microteaching. It could reveal something of the
students' learning in microteaching.

Using MRCIAS also revealed two facets of
students' microteaching experience that appeared
worthy of more detailed exploration. Firstly,
differences in the tutors' supervisory style focused
attention on the interpersonal relationships between
tutor and students. Secondly, the revelations that
students in microteaching were learning to see
themselves as teachers and that the review groups
felt a need to talk often about the role of
microteaching in their education suggested that a
study of the growth of the students' self-concept as
a teacher would be worthwhile. Further exploratory
studies were undertaken to try to develop ways of
investigating these two aspects of students'
learning in microteaching.

STUDYING STUDENT-TUTOR INTERPERSONAL RELATIONSHIPS

In order to explore further the interpersonal
relationships between tutors and their students and
come to some understanding of the affective
dimension of the tutor's role in microteaching a
search was made for a suitable research instrument.
Blumberg (1968) had used the Barrett-Lennard
Relationship Inventory (1962) to indicate the
quality of the interpersonal relationships that
inservice teachers on graduate courses in one
institution saw existing between themselves and
their supervisors. He was able to show that
teachers, whose supervisors used more indirect
supervisory styles, were more likely to give
positive evaluations of the quality of the
interpersonal relationships with their supervisor.

He found the Relationship Inventory to be a reliable way of measuring relationships which were supportive and which built and maintained the student's sense of personal worth and importance.

Dussault (1970) developed a theory of supervision in teacher education which regarded supervision as a form of teaching. He applied Rogers' (1957) theory of therapy and personality change and argued that the interpersonal relationships established between the student teacher and supervisor were important in facilitating changes in the student's personality and behaviour. Dussault pointed out that the Barrett-Lennard Relationship Inventory, which had been developed for therapeutic situations, could be used as an operational definition and measuring instrument for the quality of interpersonal relationships between student teacher and supervisor in teacher education. He considered that the content validity, reliability and power of discrimination of the inventory had been satisfactorily established. Walker and Little (1969) applied the inventory successfully to ask undergraduates about their relationship to some person important to them, and they also commented that the Relationship Inventory had been used in over 50 different studies.

One form of the Barrett-Lennard Relationship Inventory is a 64 item questionnaire which contains four subscales measuring the level of regard, empathetic understanding, congruence and unconditionality of regard that the client perceived in his relationship with his therapist. The regard scale measures the amount of regard as a person that one individual sees himself receiving from another. The empathy scale indicates the degree of non-valued understanding that is conveyed behaviourally from one person to another. The unconditionality of regard scale shows the degree of consistency in one person's affective response to another. The congruence scale measures interpersonal trust in that the highly congruent individual is completely honest and sincere in the meanings he conveys. Each scale contains eight positively phrased and eight negatively phrased items. Respondents are asked to rate the person under focus on each item using a rating scale of +3 to -3. The Relationship Inventory yields four subscale totals, though in applying it to the supervision of teachers Blumberg had used only a total score, assuming that this would give a gross measure of teachers' perceptions of the quality of their interpersonal relationships with their supervisors.

Could the Barrett-Lennard Relationship Inventory be used to measure the interpersonal relationships between student teachers and their tutors in microteaching? McGarvey and Harris carried out a series of investigations over three years, 1975-77, to answer this question. In the first of these investigations 39 students completed the Relationship Inventory and the results were subjected to item analysis. The internal consistency reliability coefficient (Cronbach's alpha) for the total inventory was high at 0.91, but values of 0.63 and 0.64 obtained for the subscales empathy and unconditionality of regard were less satisfactory. A number of items were identified as being problematic in that the item analysis showed that they failed to discriminate between respondents who obtained high and low scores on the total and subscale scores. The results obtained from this small group were considered sufficiently acceptable to proceed to develop the inventory for application to microteaching.

The wording of some items was altered in order to refer more directly to students' feelings towards their tutor in the microteaching context. A Likert-type rating scale was introduced to simplify the self-report response format. Students were asked to indicate on a 5-point scale how strongly they felt that each item was true or not true of their relationship with their tutor. A trial was conducted with 116 students and inventory items which performed poorly were identified and eliminated. Another trial was then carried out with 98 students responding to the revised inventory and the results were analysed and further modifications made. The techniques used in these refinements of the inventory were item analysis and factor analysis. It was found that the constructs, as represented by the Barrett-Lennard subscales, were very closely inter-related when applied to the student-tutor relationships in microteaching and that it was not possible to distinguish them clearly. The inventory in its new form was best regarded as one coherent scale yielding only a total score. The final version of the inventory that emerged from these trials was a 54 item scale, the Student Relationship Inventory (Appendix B).

In a later test of this inventory responses were obtained from 148 students. Item analysis of this data gave very satisfactory results with internal consistency reliability of 0.94 and with no further items being rejected. The Student Relationship Inventory was deemed suitable as a research instrument to study the affective relationships of students with their tutors in microteaching review conferences.

STUDYING STUDENTS' SELF-CONCEPT AS TEACHER

Since the initial investigations had indicated that students were learning much from microteaching besides improving the performance of their teaching skills, it was decided to see if it would be possible to obtain a measure of the contribution that microteaching was making to the students' growth into teachers. In learning to be teachers students need to change gradually their view of themselves through having experiences which build positive self-evaluations. Teacher education challenges students to discover and understand themselves as teachers. They need to come to view teaching and learning as sensitive interactive processes and to value such qualities of the effective teacher as empathy, warmth and genuineness. They need to develop conviction about their own value system for teaching and confidence in their own capabilities as teachers.

How is microteaching helping students develop their self-concept as teacher? In order to explore this question McGarvey and Harris developed a self-report attitude scale over the three year period 1975 to 1977. The scale sought to gauge students' feelings about their progress towards being a teacher and how microteaching aided or hindered this development. A useful starting point was Waetjen's (1963) Self-concept as Learner Scale, which measures four dimensions of the learner's self-concept: motivation, task orientation, problem solving and class membership. The motivation and task orientation dimensions seemed applicable to students learning to be teachers in the microteaching context, and the class membership dimension could be replaced by the microteaching peer group membership. Also, Soare and Soare (1968, 1974) had investigated the congruence between student teachers' self-concepts and their views as to how their supervisors and cooperating teachers on teaching practice saw them. They found that the students' self-concepts were similar to the ratings they thought their supervisors would give but highly

47

dissimilar to how they thought the cooperating teachers saw them. No details of the research instrument were given. Soare and Soare interpreted their results to suggest that the supervisor had greater impact than the cooperating teacher on the development of the students' self-concept in a teaching role. This view supported the findings of our own observation studies that the supervisor was very influential in microteaching. Hence a supervision dimension was considered an essential part of the scale. The initial observation studies had also revealed that the review groups sometimes spent considerable time in discussing how the microteaching system was functioning as an educational context. It was considered important to ask students how they felt the technology of microteaching was helping them develop as teachers. How did they react to the pressures of being observed and recorded and how were these pressures felt to affect their development? Another construct of seeming importance in making learning progress in teaching was that of competence. Did students feel they were gaining confidence in their teaching abilities in microteaching? Did they see themselves as working to the best of their abilities? Did they perceive that they were progressing successfully? In all, six dimensions were considered to contribute to students' development as teachers through microteaching: motivation, task orientation, group membership, supervision, competence and the microteaching context itself.

Taking suitable items from Waetjens' subscales of motivation, task orientation and group membership and adding many more new items designed to have face validity for the dimensions identified, gave a bank of initial items. This listing included both positively and negatively orientated items and was subjected to repeated trials and modifications using item analysis and factor analysis procedures. The task orientated sub-scale was found to overlap substantially with the competence and motivation sub-scales and was absorbed into these two sub-scales. The eventual outcome was the Self-concept as Teacher Scale, which consisted of 45 items in 5 subscales (motivation, competence, microteaching context, supervision and peer group influence).

The final version of the scale was tested again and 151 out of 157 students responded (96%). The internal consistency reliability for the measures obtained was 0.91 and no further items were

rejected. The Self-concept as Teacher Scale
(Appendix C) was thus acceptable as a research
instrument which would show how the various
constructs it contained were influencing students'
feelings about their personal development as
teachers in microteaching.

CONCLUSIONS

These exploratory investigations have described some
of the features of the microteaching system in
operation at the New University of Ulster. Methods
have been developed by which those aspects of
microteaching which seem worthy of close scrutiny
can be investigated. The decision to undertake
descriptive studies rather than experimental studies
has been justified. The assumptions in the
literature about what students learn from
microteaching have been shown to be open to serious
question. Comparative research studies had focused
too quickly on 'how well' students learn without
paying sufficient attention to 'what' they actually
learn. Clearly, they were learning much besides the
ability to perform selected teaching skills, and
further descriptive studies were needed to tease out
the learning processes operating in microteaching
and their underlying constructs.
          The supervision of microteaching appeared to
be a particularly important feature of the New
University of Ulster system because of the tutor's
role as examiner and the freedom that the tutor had
in defining his supervisory role. How does the
supervisor perceive microteaching? What approaches
does he employ? What does he wish his students to
achieve from microteaching? In order to research
these questions and the set of issues outlined above
a detailed study of supervision was required. First,
a review of the literature of supervision in teacher
education was carried out to identify the variety of
approaches to supervision that have been advocated,
and the supervisory strategies that have been
adopted.

Chapter 3

A REVIEW OF SUPERVISION IN TEACHER EDUCATION

A review of the literature was undertaken in 1977 to
identify the various conceptualisations of
supervision that had been applied in teacher
education. The purpose of this review was to judge
the suitability of these conceptualisations as
reference frameworks for investigations of
supervision in microteachng. Two main sources of
views on supervision were found concerning the
supervision of teachers and student teachers in
schools and the supervision of microteaching.

THE SUPERVISION OF TEACHERS IN SCHOOLS

Supervision as Teaching
Dussault (1970) reviewed the literature on
supervision as teaching in teacher education from
1931 to 1968 and extracted a very comprehensive and
useful series of inventories of the characteristics,
phenomena and relationships that had been observed
or postulated to exist in this field. He produced
"a paradigm for supervision as teaching in teacher
education programs" (p.107) to summarise his
findings and interpretations of the relationships
between the various control, independent and
dependent variables within the supervisory
conference. Dussault classified the independent
variables into four groups in accordance with their
meaning:

    Managerial-directional meaning, as indicated by
    administrative and procedural matters, such as
    directing and leading comments that set the
    context for discussion;

    Affective meaning, concerning the personal

50

relationships between the supervisor and the
supervisee(s);

Substantive meaning, regarding the content of
the conference discussion;

Cognitive-logical meaning, associated with the
supervisory procedures, i.e. -what the
supervisor did in the form of supervision in
order to promote learning.

Concentrating on the affective meaning
generated within the conference and its implied
outcomes, and using Rogers' (1957, 1959) theory of
therapy and personality change, Dussault developed a
theory of supervision in teacher education
laboratories. He suggested that the nature of the
relationship between tutor and students was an
important factor in achieving those teaching
objectives concerned with the development of
students' self-concept and self-evaluation as
teacher.

Supervision as Instruction
Alfonso, Firth and Neville (1975) developed a theory
of Instructional Supervisory Behaviour, which was
defined as:

behavior officially designated by the
organisation that directly affects teacher
behavior in such a way as to facilitate pupil
learning and achieve the goals of the
organisation. (p.36)

Alfonso, Firth and Neville were considering the
supervision of teachers working in their schools.
They took account of the various theories concerned
with the way individuals react and interrelate
within organisations and considered their
implications for educational supervision which they
regarded as a highly skilled activity. The purpose
of supervision was declared to be the promotion of
those conditions which would help the organisation
achieve its goals, so the theory of Instructional
Supervisory Behaviour was organisation orientated
rather than teacher orientated. They viewed the
supervisor as providing instructional leadership and
producing purposeful change in teacher behaviour in
order to improve learning. They considered
supervision to depend upon the supervisor's personal
qualities, his interaction with other members of the

organisation and the environmental conditions that characterised that organisation. They outlined the technical skills which they believed the supervisor needed to use in order to intervene to influence teacher behaviour.

Supervision as Counselling
Goldhammer (1969) argued that an exclusive focus on the substantive and technical elements of instruction would only result in transient behavioural changes. He valued the teacher's autonomy and highlighted the uniqueness of an individual's teaching performance, each lesson having an intensely personal flavour, arising out of the teacher's particular viewpoint of the world in which he lived. He suggested that what was being presented during a teaching encounter was more than a standard content curriculum; it was a lesson dealing with a person's self-experience, his attitudes acting as dynamic variables affecting the learning experience. It was the teacher's emotional capacities, his cognitive styling, his view of life and the world, his values, the terms in which he had learned to meet anxiety - in short - his human capacities, which were the essence of all his teaching.

He proposed a form of supervision, clinical supervision, in which the supervisor acted as counsellor. The terms used to describe the ideal situation in clinical supervision were intimacy, understanding, mutual trust, openness, spontaneous authentic affection, and empathy. Its principal aim was to sensitise the teacher to feelings, thereby increasing the potential of the supervisory conference to help personalise the teacher's relationship with children. Clinical supervision was essentially analytical, making sense out of observations through detailed examination of teaching behaviours and it involved a process in which teachers were invited to evaluate their own teaching within their own experiential frameworks. The focus of enquiry was orientated towards the teacher's own issues, with supervisory goal setting occurring primarily within the teacher's own frame of reference.

Supervision as a Social System
Like Goldhammer, Blumberg (1974) emphasised the idiosyncratic nature of teaching, stating that for supervision to be effective the individual differences that existed between teachers needed to

be acknowledged. Blumberg considered that the supervisory process involved collaborative problem solving and that this developed best when the supervisee experienced a relationship with his supervisor which involved "communicative openness" and an atmosphere of "colleagueship". This relationship, Blumberg argued, would show that the supervisor valued the student's "worth as a person" by giving him the "personal independence and freedom" to take responsibility for his own "personal and professional growth". This sense of his "own professional competence" would give the student the confidence to accept helpful suggestions from his supervisor, even though they might be aimed at weaknesses in the observed teaching.

This student would sense that his supervisor would provide "support for risk taking" and would feel encouraged to explore the boundaries of his teaching and attempt alternative approaches. In these circumstances, warned Blumberg, when failure occured this should not be construed as a sign of incompetence; rather, the teacher should be encouraged in what after all was a new venture.

Conclusions

This review of the conceptualisations of supervision in teacher education, with particular reference to the supervisory conference, has identified those perspectives that appear relevant to the supervision of microteaching. In fact, Dussault's theory includes the other conceptualisations within its four aspects of the supervisory conference.

1. The affective meaning referred to the interpersonal relationship between the supervisor and the student teacher. This has been exemplified by considering supervision to be counselling. Clinical supervision emphasised the need to build the kind of rapport that was based on trust.

2. The cognitive-logical meaning referred to the procedures adopted by the supervisor. This has been exemplified by viewing supervision as a social system as exemplified by Blumberg's collaborative problem solving approach.

3. The managerial-directional meaning concerned the supervisor's leadership role.

4. The substantive meaning referred to the

discussion content. Both managerial-directional and substantive meanings could be exemplified by viewing supervision as instruction, as advocated by Alfonso et al.

Another reason for favouring Dussault's theory was that his view of supervision as essentially a teaching role fitted well with our preliminary observations and descriptions of microteaching supervisors at work.

THE SUPERVISION OF MICROTEACHING

Conceptualisations of the supervision of microteaching have been rare, most studies having been concerned with surveying the varied functions of the supervisor (Griffiths, 1972; Gibbs, 1973; Brown, 1975b) or with researching (Shivley, Van Mondfrans & Reed, 1970; Perrott, 1972) or reviewing (Griffiths, 1975; Perrott, 1977) the effectiveness of supervisory feedback. Bibliographies on the supervision of microteaching have been published by McAleese and Unwin, 1973; Parry and Gibbs, 1974; and Parry, 1977.

Griffiths (1974) noted that a common failing of studies of microteaching supervision was their lack of specificity as to the details of the supervision provided. In a later paper, Griffiths (1976) concluded:

After gross analysis, three different conceptualisations can be identified... firstly... an approach to supervision related to the behaviouristic theory of 'shaping'... secondly, formulation of the supervisor's contribution in terms of a counselling role is possible... thirdly, a perspective on supervision might be developed from an approach which focused on cognitive variables in the critique situation... Evidence of the comparative effectiveness of supervisors working on the basis of these conceptualisations is, however, unavailable... it appears necessary to rely upon an eclectic listing of possible and overlapping supervisor tasks...(p.12)

Supervision would appear to have two dimensions that need to be taken into account. There is the approach adopted and the strategies used for its implementation. The supervisor's aims, as expressions of his aspirations and ideals, provide the rationale for the supervisory approach adopted. The choice of strategies by which the supervisory approach is implemented is dependent upon the sensitivity and skills of the tutor and the conceptualisations that are most helpful in describing this aspect of supervision are those of Dussault and Goldhammer. Thus Griffiths' second conceptualisation, supervision as counselling, may be regarded as part of this second dimension, which is concerned with the affective meaning and interpersonal relationships that are fostered.

Bearing in mind the differing conceptualisations of microteaching outlined in Chapter One, the following supervisory approaches appear reasonable.

The Behaviour Modification Approach
The original conception of microteaching at Stanford University was based on behaviour modification principles and was characterised by an emphasis on perceptual modelling, very short lessons, and one or more reteach sessions. Supervisory feedback (Koran, 1969; St. John-Brooks and Spelman, 1973) was concerned with shaping specific teaching behaviour.

> The student attempts to approximate the teaching behaviour of a model which has been presented to him. The supervisor provides feedback - information as to the degree of success the student has achieved in his imitation. In accordance with behaviourist theory, if a student receives positive feedback, he will continue to teach in the same manner...(St. John-Brooks and Spelman, 1973)

However, in implementing this approach account was taken of the need to create an encouraging atmosphere in which the students' confidence and their perceptions of the skills were developed. To this end, Allen and Ryan (1969), Olivero (1970) and McAleese and Unwin (1971) viewed the microteaching supervisor also playing important roles as a person sensitive to differences among students, an adviser and resource person for information on curriculum and methods, an interpreter of student feedback, and a general morale booster.

The Problem Solving Approach
The act of problem solving may be regarded as having

three distinct phases labelled by Borton (1970,
p.88) as "What?", "So what?", and "Now what?". The
"What?" phase concerned information, the "sensing
out of response, actual effect, and intended
effect". The "So what?" phase concerned analysis,
the process of "transforming that information into
immediately relevant patterns of meaning". The "Now
what?" phase concerned suggestion, where decisions
were made on "how to act out the best alternative
and reapply it in other situations".

Blumberg identified two strategies for a
problem solving approach to supervision. A 'direct'
supervisory strategy emphasised telling,
criticising, and suggesting the means of
improvement, whereas an 'indirect' strategy employed
reflecting, and the asking for information, opinions
and ways of avoiding certain difficulties in the
future. These indirect and direct strategies had
been taken into account in developing the MRCIAS
observation system. The essential difference
between them was the open or closed nature of the
discussions with regard to valuing students' views
or providing tutor's views. In other words they
differed in the affective meaning and relationships
within the group.

Thus a problem solving approach visualised
microteaching as a scaled down classroom practice
situation in which particular problems were
identified and analysed following each teaching
encounter so that suggestions for improvement
emerged and could be implemented in subsequent
microlessons.

The Cognitive Approach
Griffiths has offered a conceptualisation of
supervision that focused on facilitating students'
cognitive development as opposed to one that
concentrated exclusively on teaching behaviour.
This approach to supervision was derived from the
cognitive interpretation of microteaching (MacLeod
and McIntyre, 1977; Griffiths, 1977) which has been
described in Chapter One. Griffiths suggested that
a cognitive approach would be orientated towards
using the students' experiences of teaching the
microlesson and the viewing of the videorecording to
analyse how and why events occurred. The thrust in
cognitive supervision was towards analysis, not
suggestion as in a problem solving approach,
although some problem solving would be necessary in
the case of a student experiencing serious
difficulties. However, in suggesting a cognitive

interpretation of microteaching supervision,
Griffiths does not appear to have taken into account
the affective meaning inherent in the supervisory
conference.

As with problem solving, two different
strategies for a cognitive approach to supervision
seem possible. In the first strategy, the
supervisor may view himself as the expert with the
experience, ability, and qualities of perception to
identify issues worthy of discussion that have
arisen out of students' lessons and to relate these
to a general understanding of teaching. The task of
the inexperienced student would be to develop his
own cognitive schemata of teaching from listening to
the analysis and critique provided by the
experienced tutor. An alternative strategy would be
to argue that what matters primarily is what the
student thinks, since it is he who is developing his
own conceptual framework for teaching. The
objective of supervision would then be to influence
the student's perceptions of teaching and not to
impose the supervisor's own model of teaching. This
would require the tutor to value an open strategy
for the supervisory conference using indirect
procedures to encourage his students to express
their own experiences and perceptions of teaching.
The student would be supported and encouraged in
identifying and analysing aspects of teaching in the
videotaped microlessons in order to argue out his
own framework of concepts for thinking about his
teaching.

Conclusions
It has been proposed that the supervision of
microteaching may be regarded as consisting of two
dimensions. The first dimension concerns the
approach to supervision and stems from the
supervisor's personal aims and the institution's
aims for microteaching. Three approaches have been
described. The Behaviour Modification Approach
originates in a technical skills model of
microteaching. The Problem Solving Approach is
associated with an integrated skills perspective
that employs microteaching as a scaled-down teaching
practice, allowing greater controls than are
possible during school practice. The Cognitive
Approach is derived from a conceptualisation of
microteaching that views the development of
students' cognitive schemata as a prerequisite to
changes in teaching behaviour.

The second dimension concerns the affective

meaning within the supervisory conference and may be
regarded as the facilitating atmosphere or enabling
mechanism by which the tutor achieves his aims.
Associated with this dimension are the relationships
existing between the supervisor and the students,
and the indirect/direct strategies adopted by the
supervisor. These two dimensions are inter-related
and both must be considered in researching
microteaching supervision. These dimensions are
summarised in Figure 3.1.

Fig. 3.1: Conceptualising microteaching supervision

DIMENSION 1:   SUPERVISORY APPROACH

    A. The Behaviour Modification Approach
    B. The Problem-Solving Approach
    C. The Cognitive Approach

DIMENSION 2:   AFFECTIVE MEANING

    associated with -
  (i) supervisor-student affective relations
 (ii) indirect/direct supervisory procedures

Chapter 4.

A CASE STUDY OF MICROTEACHING

It was evident from the reviews of the different
conceptualisations and practices of microteaching
and its supervision and from the preliminary
research into the nature of microteaching at the New
University of Ulster that individual students could
take very different learning gains from
microteaching and that supervision was a major
influence on the type of learning gains that were
made. One interesting aspect of McIntyre, MacLeod
and Griffiths' (1977) report from Stirling
University was the section in which four curriculum
staff from Science, English, Modern Languages and
History presented their views and experiences of
microteaching. What was clear from the four papers,
and the preliminary discussion by the editors, was
that different approaches to and understanding of
microteaching existed.

     What was microteaching at the New University of
Ulster? Did all supervisors regard it as the same
thing? What commonality existed concerning
objectives and approach? A clear and penetrating
description of microteaching in action was needed
and in order to provide this description Swallow
(1984) carried out a case study of microteaching
over the three year period 1977-80.

THE AIMS OF THE MICROTEACHING SUPERVISORS

The first step was to find out what exactly were the
aims for microteaching which the tutors held. This
would enable consensus and conflicting views to be
identified and would indicate the attitudes and
approaches that supervisors valued in their efforts
to achieve their aims. What were the criteria by
which decisions were made? How did tutors employ

their skills as supervisors to shape the processes
inherent in microteaching? What were their personal
constructs for microteaching? It was decided to
interview all the microteaching tutors to elicit
their personal constructs (Kelly, 1955, 1970) for
microteaching.

A personal construct system implies:

> a personal construction or representation of
> some aspect of reality that is the result of an
> individual's interpretation of his world...and
> is the means by which (he will) predict and
> anticipate events, as a forerunner to action
> (Bussis, Chittenden and Amarel, 1976, p.16).

Bussis et al. in their interview study of
teachers' understandings placed great importance on
the ability of teachers to see connections between
their "surface curriculum" (what they did in the
classroom) and their "organising priorities" (their
educational aims for the children). They regarded
these connections not only as the means by which
teachers communicated their rationale to others, but
also as the basis of their evaluations of their
teaching. In interviewing the microteaching
supervisors, the research sought to move beyond
tutors' "surface curriculum" in order to investigate
the kinds of connections to which Bussis referred.

Methodology

The interview approach adopted and the means by
which the resulting interpretations were achieved
were grounded in the principles of an illuminative
methodology (Hamilton et al, 1977). While the
earlier exploratory researches and reviews have
yielded a developing understanding of microteaching
and its supervision, it needs be stressed that this
background work did not form the basis for an 'a
priori' classification of aims.

> Here lies a major difference between the
> traditional evaluator and his illuminative
> counterpart. The former stimulates
> participants' responses by using standardised
> tests and pre-planned interview schedules. The
> illuminative evaluator, in contrast, allows the
> participants to stimulate evaluation responses.
> (Dearden and Laurillard, 1977, p.3)

The interviewer was determined not to offer
alternatives, but to probe for the tutors' learning

priorities and the kinds of connections they were making with the many process variables in microteaching. The interview timetable was purposely very intense, in order that ideas would grow and develop in the transition from one interview to the next. The interviews averaged around thirty-five minutes and were audiotaped and subsequently transcribed. Post interview impressions were written down immediately following each interview as a concise synthesis of what were believed to be the emerging issues. The maturation process involved in moving from one interview to the next was a most important aspect of the tutor interviews. As such, the whole time period in which the interviews took place was experienced as an intense mental activity in which the formulation and reformulation of the emergent issues was a very interactive and educative process for the researcher. All 27 staff who acted as microteaching supervisors in the 1977/78 programme were interviewed, the vast majority of whom were known to the researcher. Upon reflection, it is considered that the fact that the interviewer was not a stranger in the institution but had progressed through the system as an undergraduate helped to pave the way towards the kind of frank and honest exchanges necessary for this type of in-depth interviewing.

Macleod, Griffiths and McIntyre (1977b) had compared the effects of three microteaching treatments on students' subsequent teaching behaviour and had reported that students' use of the skills involved in the study appeared to be closely related to their subject specialisms. Macleod and McIntyre (1977) also commented:

> One might interpret this in terms of the different demands and opportunities involved in teaching different subjects, although it should also be noted that different subject specialists in the Stirling department vary in their enthusiasm for microteaching. (p.115)

Consequently, tutors' teaching interests were kept in mind throughout this research as a potential influence on their aims and supervisory behaviour. Supervisors were classified as either Educational Studies tutors, or Curriculum Methods tutors. Educational Studies tutors lectured in Educational Psychology, Sociology and Philosophy, while Curriculum Methods tutors specialised in the

curriculum study of Language and Creative Arts,
Environmental Science, Mathematics, or the Sciences.
In drawing together the threads of the
interviews, it was apparent that there was a range
of issues about which tutors were in general
agreement. There were also some major contrasting
views being expressed which could be broadly grouped
into four approaches to microteaching.

Consensus Views

Tutors confirmed that a principal aim was to give
students some introductory, thought provoking
experiences of meeting children in the role of
teacher. However the microteaching system was seen
to offer opportunities to do much more than this and
it is in achieving these other aims that supervision
was considered to be an influential task. In this
respect all tutors considered supervision to be a
relevant and important dimension of microteaching.
Tutors were very sensitive to the fact that they
were acting in relative isolation from each other
and from the lecture programme. Many expressed a
strong interest to know of the aims and approaches
that others favoured and the reasons behind their
views.

Tutors considered the working relationships and
atmosphere that the group developed were important,
with an open, communicative and supportive
relationship being sought. Supervisors who had more
than one group remarked that the relationships which
developed in their paralled groups were very
different, being dependent on the interest, ability
and personalities of the students. This was not
surprising, but what was interesting was that, while
supervisors claimed to alter their strategy, they
appeared to hold true to their aims. Thus they
tended to see supervision as a dominant influence,
determining to a large extent what students gained
from microteaching.

Tutors regarded their role as examiner to be a
restrictive influence in establishing the rapport
which they desired, and they used a variety of
strategies to play down assessment. Some kept
assessment as something separate, taking place after
microteaching. Thus the final two assessed lessons
were not accompanied by review conferences. Others
held that these last lessons were still valuable
learning experiences and there was much to be gained
by discussing them. They adopted a very open
approach to assessment throughout the unit and not
just in the final weeks. Students were continually

assured that they were progressing satisfactorily,
that they were going to pass, and that assessment
could be set aside in order to concentrate on the
learning experiences.

Without exception, tutors had rejected the
original Stanford Model of microteaching. They
regarded the isolation of specific teaching
behaviours and their modification through practice
as totally unrealistic. Teaching was seen to be a
complex integrated activity in which behaviour
always had a context which was related to precedent
and antecedent events. The main aim of supervision
was declared to be prompting students toward
self-discovery by encouraging the development of the
skills of perception and interpretation of
significant events in teaching encounters. Through
self-evaluation and discussion of the teaching
performance of peers, students should be helped
develop their own appropriate and individualistic
teaching style.

Contrasting Views
Although tutors in general subscribed to these
consensus views they differed markedly in the
subsidiary aims which they considered went toward
achieving this ultimate goal. In the following
attempt to identify characteristic viewpoints and to
group similar aims through a classificatory
framework it needs to be remembered that
supervision, like teaching, is a complex integrated
activity, upon which a classification system is
being imposed. The approaches to be described have
been identified as characteristic of supervisors'
aims, though they cannot be regarded as being
totally discrete; rather, they are useful guidelines
for discussing supervision. While supervisors would
see themselves as being predominantly of one
described category they would certainly recognise
within themselves elements of the other
classifications.

Aims were classified as to whether they were
concerned primarily with the practice of teaching or
with the integration of the theory and practice of
teaching. The Practice for Classroom Teaching
Approach aimed at helping students develop
competence in the performance of teaching through
overcoming those difficulties which had been
highlighted by focused review of the videorecording.
This was a problem-solving enterprise with the
identification and analysis of difficulties leading
to specific suggestions for improvement. Two

sub-categories were identified and designated IA, Problem Solving for Teaching Skills and IB, Problem Solving for Teaching Practice. The former was characterised by the tutor's willingness to conform to what he or she believed to be the role prescribed by the programme structure, whereas the latter viewed microteaching mainly as practice teaching, so that microteaching was a first practice preparing the way for the second practice in schools.

Those tutors who professed themselves to be more interested in developing an understanding of teaching by seeking to integrate theoretical and practical considerations concentrated on prompting students to ask themselves, through evaluating their experiences, 'What is teaching really about?'. The essential aim was to help students build their own conceptual model of teaching, i.e. a Teacher Concept Development Approach. Again these aims could be classified into two categories, those emphasising teaching as providing learning experiences - designated IIA, Teaching Concept Development - learning experiences orientated; and those emphasising teaching as creating a desirable learning climate through appropriate teacher-pupil relationships - designated IIB, Teaching Concept Development - relationships orientated.

The characteristics of these four approaches to the supervision of microteaching are now outlined.

The Practice for Classroom Teaching Approach

IA, Problem Solving for Teaching Skills The knowledge that the lecture programme was dealing with specific skills, and the concrete evidence of this that was provided by the skill rating schedules, promoted a professional commitment on the part of these tutors to study the 'weekly skill' under consideration and to provide an integrated experience for the student by linking lecture programme and review conference. However, while the skill of the week was considered, it was not handled in a behaviour modification manner as in the Stanford model, but was treated as one component of the global skills of teaching. The opportunities that the videorecording and review conference provided were taken to consider the wider range of global skills in a problem solving manner.

The focus was very definitely on skills and students were encouraged to analyse their performance so that suggestions for change emerged. In this respect tutors were interested in tackling real problems, so it was important that the

microteaching experience resembled classroom
situations as closely as possible. However it was
not considered necessary to have long microlessons.
The short microlesson was considered sufficient to
demonstrate a range of skills, and was advantageous
in sharpening focus on specific skills identified as
problematic.

The majority of tutors considered that they had
moved on from this approach. They argued that
students were much too inexperienced to plan a
lesson which allows practice of a specific skill,
and that teaching was a more interesting and more
complex construct than the sum of its component
skills would indicate.

IB, Problem Solving for Teaching Practice Tutors
who favoured this approach considered that the main
advantages of microteaching over teaching practice
were that first attempts at teaching were made in a
low risk situation and that a videorecording of the
complete lesson was available for review.
Microteaching, as first steps in teaching, was aimed
at allowing students to develop performance
competencies which would give them a 'head start' in
teaching practice. In this respect it was
considered important that microteaching should
present situations which were as similar as possible
to those in the classroom and that students should
use their experiences and reviews of their own and
their peers' lessons to improve their performance.
An appropriate approach to achieving this was a
problem solving one in which specific problems and
shortcomings were identified in the lessons taught,
discussed and suggestions made for improvement.

Such tutors desired long lessons "more like the
usual thirty-five minute periods in secondary
schools" and more pupils, including opportunities to
teach secondary school pupils, in order to alleviate
the 'artificiality' of microteaching. They also
reacted against the behaviouristic bias of the
lectures and rating schedules, assuming (wrongly)
that a behaviour modification model for
microteaching was implied. Accordingly, little
notice was taken of the lectures or of the 'skill of
the week'.

Favouring a teaching performance model and a
problem-solving approach meant that some of these
tutors found microteaching an unreal and frustrating
exercise. The difficulty was that the inexperience
of the students, the artificiality of the
environment and the special skills required of

students to produce short 'unreal' lessons,
conspired together to present students with so many
problems that this did not seem an appropriate way
of beginning to practise teaching. From this
viewpoint an argument was made that students would
get much more out of microteaching if they had some
preliminary experience in classrooms. This in turn
presented tutors with a chicken/egg paradox as to
the relationship between microteaching and classroom
teaching.

The Teaching Concept Development Approach

Many tutors considered the Practice for Classroom
Teaching Approach to be inappropriate because the
students did not have a conceptual framework to
which they could relate their experiences. They saw
the main thrust of supervision in microteaching
being to help students perceive and interpret their
experiences, thereby developing an understanding of
the teaching process. In this way students would be
in a better position to benefit from teaching
practice because they should be able to evaluate
their own teaching performance, identify their own
problems and seek self-improvement. Some tutors had
arrived at this approach to microteaching by
thought-out decisions, others had adopted it by
reacting spontaneously to their own experiences,
while others had been forced to this position, being
problem solvers at heart, but finding problem
solving to be a second order process requiring as
prerequisite a framework of concepts to apply in
problem solving.

This view of microteaching suggested that
students were learning as much about themselves as
they were about teaching. Students were encouraged
to explore their feelings of "myself as teacher".
The in-depth analysis of review conference
discussions depended not only on the interest and
ability of the students but also on the atmosphere
in which these discussions took place. Tutors were
very sensitive to the need to establish an
appropriate working relationship with students in
which the affective climate in the group was just as
important as the cognitive issues discussed.

The lecture programme was regarded as being
helpful in that it elucidated one aspect of teaching
and provided a common language for talking about
teaching. But this was only one of many aspects so
the 'skill of the week' was treated lightly, if at
all, in review conferences. Tutors wanted short
microlessons, requiring a 'quick turnaround'

learning environment for students. Two fifteen
minute lessons were considered to be much more
beneficial than one thirty minute lesson. A fifteen
minute lesson was sufficiently long to focus on
interesting opportunities to learn about "What is
actually going on here?". Also the bombardment
effect of many interesting happenings within a
thirty minute lesson created a problem in that only
a few of them could be discussed and analysed
afterwards. One difficulty that these tutors
acknowledged about short lessons was the cumulative
effect on the pupils who wilted noticeably towards
the end of the session of eight microlessons.
Students who taught early in the sequence had a very
different experience of pupils from those who came
later.

**IIA, Teaching Concept Development - Learning
Experiences Orientated** As well as being concerned
with the analysis of how the students were teaching,
the tutors who advocated this approach were very
concerned with what the pupils were being taught.
The centre of the analysis was the lesson as a
genuine worthwhile learning experience for the
pupils. They argued that teaching skills were
facilitating mechanisms for learning and, as such,
were best discussed in the context of lesson
structure and pupils' learning. The lesson plan was
the initial point of focus and both subject content
and the learning processes that pupils were to
experience were examined. It was in this context
that specific teaching skills were deemed first of
all to be appropriate to apply and secondly to be
well or poorly executed, so a 'skill of the week'
approach was not adopted.

Discussions were concerned with the
relationships between what was planned and what
actually happened, seeking explanations for
disparities thereby deepening understanding of the
teaching process.

**IIB, Teaching Concept Development - Relationships
Orientated** Other tutors, who valued microteaching
as a means of exploring the 'self-concept as
teacher', regarded the lesson content and structure
as relatively unimportant because microteaching was
a laboratory environment and lesson planning as a
teaching skill needed a true classroom environment.
The laboratory environment was helpful in learning
about oneself and the way in which one interacted
with pupils as a teacher. The aim was to analyse

and understand the way the student taught in terms of the communicative atmosphere which was created and the relationships which were built with the children. As a result students should become sensitised to the effects of their teaching thereby raising some fundamental issues about 'What is teaching?', 'What am I as a teacher trying to do?' The ultimate aim was to help students create for themselves suitable frames of reference to know themselves as teachers, to be aware of their own strengths and weaknesses, and to build their own programme of improvement over many years through critical self-evaluation as they developed and tried to implement their own value systems for teaching and learning.

A Comparison of Approaches

While both the Practice for Classroom Teaching (PCT) and the Teaching Concept Development (TCD) Approaches aimed at helping students develop appropriate individualistic teaching styles they approached this aim by very different routes. The PCT Approach spotlighted teaching performance, the predominant thrust being to pass through analysis of performance to reach specific suggestions for change. The TCD Approach took a more open-ended view of performance, which was a means rather than an end in itself. By encouraging students to assimilate their own understanding of teaching the intention was that students would change their viewpoint and their value system so that future performance was influenced not merely by practice but by viewing performance from a changed perspective.

The PCT Approach was concerned with immediate gains from isolated, specific instances. It was about sorting out, week by week, 'what worked for you' i.e. the build-up of a repertoire of ad hoc coping behaviours. The TCD Approach aimed to build specific instances into a general picture so that wide ranging foundations of understanding were constructed for the teacher to use as the circumstances indicate. PCT tutors found microteaching artificial and restrictive, and would wish to alter the format to fit their aims more closely. The TCD tutors accepted the artificiality of microteaching. They did not regard this to be a limitation on their ability to study teaching in depth. PCT tutors wished to attain specific solutions whereas the others regarded this aim as being too limited, it being more important to help students develop a sufficient schemata of teaching concepts to handle their own difficulties.

A Classification of Tutors

Having earlier warned the reader not to regard the imposed framework as presenting totally discrete categories, it was of interest nevertheless to attempt a classification of tutors based on the predominant viewpoint that tutors expressed to the interviewer. Figure 4.1 shows a classification of tutors as seen by the interviewer. It illustrates the spread of tutors' views about the aims of microteaching.

Fig. 4.1: A classification of tutors by their aims

Predominant aims of microteaching	Ed.St. Tutors	C. M. Tutors
IA Problem Solving for Teaching Skills	2	3
IB Problem Solving for Teaching Practice	4	6
IIA Teaching Concept Development: Learning Experiences Orientated	2	2
IIB Teaching Concept Development: Relationships Orientated	5	3
TOTALS	13	14

This spread of major aims highlighted the difficulty of identifying the role of microteaching within the programme of practical studies. The essential question was, should microteaching be treated as tackling mainly short or long term aims? It would appear that staff were roughly equally divided in answering this question. In this respect microteaching was no different to any other course of study in teacher education. The balance between being relevant to students' immediate needs and

establishing a basis for continuing development
throughout a teaching career has always been a
subject of debate. Figure 4.2 summarises the
classification of tutors' aims for microteaching
that emerged from this interview research study.

Fig. 4.2: The aims of the microteaching supervisors

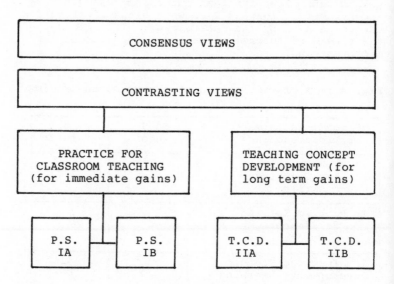

DESIGN OF THE CASE STUDY

The identification of a range of supervisory
approaches and their implications for students'
learning in microteaching provided a series of
research questions to bring to a wide-ranging and
detailed case study of microteaching in operation.
A two year study was designed with the first year,
1978/79, concentrating on obtaining a detailed
description of microteaching and the second year
extending this description and focusing in more
depth on some of the interesting outcomes of the
first year study.
     An eclectic methodology was used to follow the
experiences of students and tutors. Systematic
observation studies of the review groups were
obtained using MRCIAS and interpersonal
relationships were followed using the Student
Relationship Inventory (SRI). The Self-concept as

Teacher Scale (SCATS) gave indications of students'
feelings about their learning progress and students
were also asked to complete an open-ended
questionnaire, the Student Post Teaching
Questionnaire (Appendix D), in order to identify
their learning concerns following the microlesson
and see if the review conference discussions
addressed these issues. As well as collecting this
research data, the researcher was using an
illuminative approach, living with microteaching in
progress as a participant observer, listening with
developing sensitivity to students and staff and
writing down observations and impressions in the
ever-present field-note diary. Being there with
sensitive eyes and ears not only fleshed out the
systematic data but also provided insights into
other facets of students' and tutors' experiences.
The systematic and illuminative investigations were
planned very carefully so as not to interfere, as
far as was humanly possible, with the ongoing
microteaching programme.

The first year investigations
A number of themes was available around which to
pose questions and plan an investigative structure
for the research. These themes concerned the nature
of the supervision, the affective relationships
between students and tutors, the students'
experiences and the nature of their learning gains.
The research questions were probed by conducting
three inter-related studies which were combined into
one investigation by an appropriate design for
sampling and timing of data collection.

Study 1: A description of supervision Descriptions
of supervision were obtained by recording and
analysing review conference verbal behaviours. The
stability of the supervisors' behaviours and the
relation of these behaviours to the supervisors'
declared aims were examined. Was there stability in
tutors' verbal behaviours from occasion to occasion?
Were there characteristic differences among tutors
in their behaviours? What relationship, if any,
existed between the tutors' aims and their verbal
behaviours? How were tutors' behaviours perceived
by their students? Was there a relationship between
tutors' verbal behaviours and students' feelings
about their learning progress?
The verbal behaviours of a stratified sample of
review groups were collected on two occasions and
were systematically analysed for content of

discussion and interaction style using MRCIAS. This investigation was designed as a longitudinal study over two years so that comparisons could be made of different groups who had the same tutor. The verbal behaviours were compared with the tutors' aims and declared approach as elicited earlier by interview. Students' feelings about their learning were obtained on two occasions using the Self-concept as Teacher Scale (SCATS) to see if any changes could be detected and related to supervisors' behaviours. A stratified sample of students was interviewed on two occasions immediately following their review conferences in order to obtain their perceptions of their supervisors' behaviours.

Study 2: Affective meaning in the review conferences

It was suggested in Chapter Three that supervision could be regarded as consisting of two dimensions, the supervisory approach and the affective meaning, or facilitating atmosphere, existing within the review conference. In particular, Teaching Concept Development tutors had emphasised that they valued an indirect approach to their supervision, their purpose being to provide an atmosphere which would support students as they developed their personal models for teaching. The indirect/direct strategies adopted by the tutor and both tutors' and students' perceptions of the interpersonal relationships within the review conference were investigated. Did Teaching Concept Development tutors differ from Practice for Classroom Teaching tutors in use of indirect/direct strategies? How did students perceive the relationship with their tutor? Did any patterns emerge with regard to how different tutors were perceived? What relationship, if any, existed between students' perceptions of their tutors and their feeling about their learning progress?

The indirect/direct strategies adopted by the tutor were summarised by the MRCIAS interactive indices available from Study 1. All students were asked to complete the Student Relationship Inventory (SRI) on two occasions and a stratified sample of students was interviewed about the relationship that they had with their tutor.

How did tutors perceive the relationship with their students? How did these views compare with students' perceptions? The Student Relationship Inventory was modified to obtain tutors' views about their relationships with their students and this new instrument was provided in two forms. The Tutor Relationship Inventory - Aims (TRIA) asked tutors about the type of relationship they sought to achieve with their students and was administered to all tutors immediately prior to the commencement of the microteaching programme. The Tutor Relationship Inventory - Experiences (TRIE) asked tutors about the relationships actually experienced with their students and was administered to all tutors near the end of the programme.

Study 3: How students were learning in microteaching

Teaching Concept Development tutors had noted the uniqueness of microteaching as a context in which students could be encouraged to develop a personal understanding of teaching. MacLeod and McIntyre had suggested that such changes in students' cognitive schemata were largely derived from "students' perceptions of what actually occurs in their microteaching lessons" and that "mechanical or descriptive feedback will only have little influence on the nature of their perceptions or therefore on their subsequent teaching behaviour" (p.260). Study 3 focused on this 'lesson experience self-confrontation'. Teaching Concept Development tutors had argued that the issues discussed in the review conference should originate from the students' experiences of having taught the lesson and that they were concerned with promoting students' skills in evaluating their own teaching.

To what extent did Teaching Concept Development tutors implement their aim of focusing the review discussion on the students' own concerns and satisfactions? Did these tutors differ from Practice for Classroom Teaching tutors in this respect? What were the students' reactions to the extent to which their self-declared concerns and satisfactions (as outlined in their post teaching responses) were discussed in the review conference? Was there a change in the quality of students' post teaching responses from occasion to occasion? Were students supervised by Teaching Concept Development tutors developing better self-evaluation skills than students supervised by Practice for Classroom Teaching tutors, as indicated by the analysis of the post teaching questionnaires?

To find answers to these questions a stratified sample of students were asked to complete the open-ended Student Post Teaching Questionnaire (SPTQ) on two separate occasions immediately after teaching their lessons. This questionnaire, see Appendix D, invited students to answer the question, "How do you feel about the lesson you have just

73

taught?" Students' responses were examined, and the issues raised were identified. The recordings of the subsequent review conferences were analysed, and the extent to which a student's self-declared issues were discussed in review were expressed as a percentage of the total number of issues named by the student in the post teaching questionnaire. A stratified random sample of students was interviewed immediately after their review conferences in order to obtain their reactions to whether or not their own concerns and satisfactions had been addressed in the review conferences.

If students were developing their skills in self-evaluation then this ought to be reflected in the quality of their written responses to the open-ended Student Post Teaching Questionnaire. A system was developed for analysing the students' responses, taking into account not only the range of issues mentioned, but also the depth of analysis with which they had been examined.

Sampling and data collection The microteaching programme involved three teaching sessions in each of five laboratory classrooms every day of the week with review conferences also taking place at the same time in other viewing rooms. Because of the number of groups that were to be investigated it was not possible to provide video equipment to record the review conferences. Instead audio-recordings were made and MRCIAS was adapted to analyse these audio-recordings. Microphones were installed as permanent facilities on the ceilings of all the viewing rooms and the recording equipment was located in a separate room. All tutors and their review groups had given permission for recordings to be made. A sample of 16 out of the 27 tutors was selected as a random stratification to give 2 Educational Studies tutors and 2 Curriculum Methods tutors for each of the 4 aims categories (IA, IB, IIA, IIB). The tutors and their review groups were not told which groups were being recorded, nor were they aware of the weeks in which recordings were made.

It was Week 4 of the programme before pupils were introduced (see Figure 1.4) and two weeks were then allowed for students to become familiar with their pupils. The last two weeks were also avoided because of the focus on assessment. It was desired to take recordings, administer inventories and conduct interviews on two separate occasions and two weeks were needed to collect one complete data set.

Thus the two separate occasions were Weeks 6/7 and
9/10 of the programme.

Figure 4.3 shows how the audio-recordings,
administration of inventories and interviews were
fitted into the two repeat occasions of the overall
research design. All 27 tutors responded to the
TRIA and TRIE relationship inventories. All 144
students in the year group completed the SRI, SCATS
and SPTQ instruments twice, a two shift system being
used to cope with the post teaching questionnaire
(i.e. SPTQ1.1 and SPTQ1.2). Thus 8 groups completed
their SPTQs and had their conferences audio-recorded
in Week 6 and the other 8 groups were treated
similarly in Week 7. Two students were randomly
selected from each review group for the Student Post
Conference Interviews (SPCI) and the responses of
these 32 students to the SPTQs were also given
special attention. A three week period was needed
to conduct these interviews (i.e. SPCI1.1, SPCI1.2
and SPCI1.3) because, in some groups, a number of
days elapsed between the microlesson and the review
conference.

The second year investigations

One component of the second year investigation had
already been planned, the longitudinal study of the
stability of tutors' behaviours being a continuation
of the first year investigations. Another component
was also related to this ongoing study. How would
tutors react to feedback from the researcher about
the characteristic features of their conferences and
his interpretations of their behaviours? A third
component had emerged from the first year study as
an interesting aspect worthy of more focused
enquiry. This concerned the tutors' models for
microteaching and how their personal construct
systems for microteaching related to their practice.

Study 1: The stability of tutors' behaviours

Because of the time needed for the other studies
which were to be conducted it was not possible to
follow the review discussions of all 16 tutors who
had been observed the previous year. A different
sample of 8 tutors was chosen, randomly selecting
one tutor from each of the 8 cells of Figure 4.1.
As in the previous year all groups gave permission
to take audio-recordings and were unaware of the
sample chosen and the weeks selected for study. The
two review conferences following Lessons 3 and 4
were recorded and analysed.

Fig. 4.3: The year 1 research design

WEEK OF THE PROGRAMME	SUPERVISED MICROTEACHING	RELATIONSHIP INVENTORIES TRI	RELATIONSHIP INVENTORIES SRI	SELF-CONCEPT AS TEACHER SCALE (SCATS)	STUDENT POST-TEACHING QUESTIONNAIRE (SPTQ)	AUDIOTAPING THE REVIEW CONFERENCES	STUDENT POST-CONFERENCE INTERVIEWS (SPCI)	THE WEEKLY SKILL
1								
2								
3		TRIA						
4	1							
5	2							
6	3				SPTQ 1.1	Systematic analysis and illuminative interpretation of the review conferences of lesson 3/4 and lesson 6/7	SPCI 1.1	Teacher Liveliness
7	4			SCATS 1	SPTQ 1.2		SPCI 1.2	Pupil Reinforcement
8	5		SRI1				SPCI 1.3	Pupil Participation
9	6				SPTQ 2.1		SPCI 2.1	Questioning 1 (Fluency)
10	7	TRIE		SCATS 2	SPTQ 2.2		SPCI 2.2	Questioning 2 (Higher Order Q)
11	8		SRI2				SPCI 2.3	
12	9							

THE FIRST SUPERVISED MICROLESSONS

Study 2: Feedback to tutors about their supervision

Did tutors feel that the researcher's descriptions were fair reflections of their work? How did they interconnect these descriptions of their actions with their aims as expressed in the initial interviews? How did they react to the researcher's inferences as to the meanings of their actions? Two approaches were adopted in obtaining tutors' views. Firstly, the 8 sample tutors were interviewed in Week 5 once recordings of their review conferences had been completed. These interviews dealt specifically with each tutor's practice. Secondly, all tutors were invited to a research seminar held about six weeks after the data collection was complete and at which the general trends and interpretations were discussed. The proceedings were audio-recorded to allow the tutors' reactions to be analysed.

Study 3: Tutors' models for microteaching

The first year study had indicated that tutors had distinctive personal construct systems for microteaching which were related to their practice, which influenced what students were learning in microteaching. It was of interest to explore tutors' personal construct systems for microteaching in more depth and try to trace the origins of these constructions in their life experiences and their beliefs about education and teaching. It was evident from the first year study that the tutors worked hard in the first few weeks of microteaching to establish their approach and make clear their expectations to students. The way in which these understandings of microteaching were articulated was followed. The first 4 review conferences of the sample of 8 tutors in Study 1 were recorded and analysed. These 8 tutors were then interviewed in depth and asked to explain their behaviours in terms of their personal understandings of teaching and teacher preparation. Their students were also interviewed in their groups and asked about their tutors' aims, approach and practice.

The following chapters take each of the major research issues in turn and present overviews of the descriptive and interpretative findings which emerged from the whole two year study.

Chapter 5.

DESCRIPTIONS OF MICROTEACHING SUPERVISION

The purpose of using systematic observation to
describe microteaching supervision was to see if
characteristic features of supervisors' behaviours
could be identified, thereby distinguishing
different approaches and relating them to tutors'
aims. It was also of interest to see if students'
perceptions of their tutors' behaviours reinforced
the findings of the systematic observation. If
tutors were able to put their declared aims for
microteaching into practice then there should be
differences in supervisory approach. In particular,
it ought to be possible to distinguish tutors by
their use of indirect/direct strategies, their focus
on weekly skill and on lesson planning and their use
of analysis and suggestions for change. Tutors
classified as favouring a Practice for Classroom
Teaching Approach (PCT) had advocated a
problem-solving approach and had indicated that a
'direct' supervisory strategy would be necessary
because of the inexperience of the students. In
contrast, Teaching Concept Development (TCD) tutors
had claimed to adopt an 'indirect' strategy being
concerned about supportive interpersonal
relationships.
     A Practice for Classroom Teaching Approach
ought also to include other characteristic
behaviours. Tutors categorised as IA, Problem
Solving for Teaching Skills had said that they felt
obliged to discuss the weekly skill under focus, as
well as a wider range of skills, whereas IB, Problem
Solving for Teaching Practice tutors claimed to take
little notice of the weekly skill seeking instead to
discuss shortcomings in the lesson and in global
teaching skills and to make suggestions for
improvement. This should result in emphasis being
placed on the lesson, on global teaching skills and

on plans for future lessons.

Teaching Concept Development tutors, on the other hand, claimed to treat the 'skill of the week' lightly. They had little interest in isolating instances and seeking remedies to these specific difficulties. Rather, the approach they desired entailed considerable discussion and analysis of both the lesson taught and teaching in general, the purpose being to help the students to build their own conceptual framework for teaching. Thus the review conference should focus on the identification, analysis and discussion of quite a number and range of issues, interspersed with many probing questions designed to make the students think more analytically. There should be relatively little time spent on the discussion of suggestions for change.

Those TCD tutors who favoured a IIA, Learning Experiences Orientated Approach would want to analyse the lesson as a genuine worthwhile learning experience for the pupils. Thus their review group discussions ought to consider the lesson's subject content, plan and structure, and the pupils' reactions and responses. On the other hand, IIB, Relationships Orientated tutors regarded the lesson content and structure as relatively unimportant compared with the opportunity that microteaching provided to learn about oneself and how one interacted with children as a teacher. Again considerable analysis and probing might be expected to take place during the review session, discussions being centred on general skills and the pupils, with relatively little talk about the lesson structure and content.

In each year of the case study the researcher trained in the application of MRCIAS until satisfactory levels of consistency were attained. Trials were then conducted on recordings of review conferences available from the preliminary investigations and it was established that there was an acceptable level of agreement between the researcher and the MRCIAS originator and also that the researcher was consistent in the repeat codings of trial recordings. Scott agreement coefficients of >0.85 for the percentage use of categories in both content and interactive dimensions were set as the criterion for satisfactory training in MRCIAS.

The two batches of recordings were systematically analysed and the resulting codings were interpreted to give the percentage use of categories in both dimensions, the interaction matrix and the problem solving and interaction indices for each review conference. A reliability cross-check was carried out in both Year 1 and Year 2 studies by re-coding one review conference a second time at the end of the analysis work. In the 1978/79 study this cross-check gave Scott coefficients of 0.93 and 0.90 for the content and interactive dimensions respectively and the similar figures for the 1979/80 study were 0.95 and 0.91. Thus it was established that there was consistency of application of MRCIAS between the original investigations and these researches and also between the Year 1 and Year 2 studies.

CLUSTER ANALYSIS

The first interpretation of the data was made by searching for behaviour patterns without application of any preconceived ideas as to groupings that could emerge. On the basis of the descriptive statistical data alone the review conferences were arranged into similar groupings by cluster analysis. Following Youngman's (1979) advice about selection of appropriate methods for cluster analysis, Ward's (1963) hierarchical agglomeration method was applied. This method begins with the individual cases as characterised by a number of measures and progressively combines, or fuses, the most similar cases into groups until only one group remains. The method is 'agglomerate' in that groups or clusters are formed by accumulation and 'hierarchical' in that it is progressive and the number and composition of the clusters can be examined at any stage. The results of cluster analysis may be presented visually by plotting a graph of the error, or distance, associated with each fusion. A sudden climb in the graph shows that relatively different groups have been amalgamated, indicating that clustering immediately before that point is worthy of note. However, where there is no obvious jump in the criterion measure this in itself does not mean a poor classification. Even more detail may be obtained by the construction of a dendogram showing the successive fusions. Since the length of each horizontal branch is proportional to the increase in error associated with the subsequent fusion, classifications before long branches are of particular interest.

The choice of variables for cluster analysis exerts a more serious effect than might be imagined.

Descriptions of microteaching supervision

To illustrate this Youngman compared the results of an analysis involving seventeen attitude and ability measures to that of a later analysis in which three ability measures had been withdrawn. The coefficient of agreement, Kappa K, was reduced from 0.66 to 0.54. Youngman concluded:

> that so few measures can have such a large effect on classification does emphasise the need for extreme care in variable selection... Most of the justification for including or excluding variables should be in terms of the research hypothesis.

Taking into account Youngman's findings of the serious effects of variable selection, it was decided to carry out three cluster analyses for each occasion in each year, using as sets of variables:

1. MRCIAS content category percentages (14 variables),
2. MRCIAS problem solving and verbal interaction category percentages (12 variables),
3. MRCIAS problem solving and interaction indices (slightly modified and extended to give 17 variables).

Detailed examination of the distance plots and dendograms indicated that the four and two cluster solutions gave the clearest patterns. These cluster solutions were then compared with the tutors' teaching subjects and with their aims for microteaching. The cluster patterns did not reveal any obvious reasons for distinguishing between the behaviours of groups supervised by Curriculum Methods tutors and those supervised by Educational Studies tutors. However, there were definite cluster patterns associated with the tutors' aims classification. In general, the review conferences of Practice for Classroom Teaching tutors formed clusters distinct from those of Teaching Concept Development tutored conferences. Moreover, these clusters were found to be reasonably stable across the different cluster analyses carried out for the different sets of variables used and for the different occasions. This was found to be the case in both Year 1 and 2 studies. These findings are illustrated by Tables 5.1 and 5.2 which present the 2 cluster solutions obtained for all 32 conferences of the Year 1 study and for all 16 conferences of

Descriptions of microteaching supervision

Table 5.1: 2 cluster solution, 32 Year 1 conferences

Classification Variables	Cluster 1		Cluster 2	
	PCT IA IB	TCD IIA IIB	PCT IA IB	TCD IIA IIB
Content Category %	0 2	8 5	8 6	0 3
Interaction Category %	2 2	6 7	6 6	2 1
Interaction Indices	0 0	7 8	8 8	1 0

Table 5.2: 2 cluster solution, 16 Year 2 conferences

Classification Variables	Cluster 1		Cluster 2	
	PCT IA IB	TCD IIA IIB	PCT IA IB	TCD IIA IIB
Content Category %	0 2	4 4	4 2	0 0
Interaction Category %	0 1	3 4	4 3	1 0
Interaction Indices	0 1	4 4	4 3	0 0

the Year 2 study.

A thorough examination of the cluster patterns did not indicate any clear distinction between the behaviours of IA and IB tutored groups or between IIA and IIB tutored groups. Thus the cluster patterns generated from the MRCIAS analyses of the content and the verbal interaction behaviours of the review conference discussions reflected the stable and dominant influence of the tutors. This was found to be the case in both the Year 1 and Year 2 studies. The overall result confirmed the existence of a relationship between a group's verbal behaviours and the aims of its microteaching supervisor in terms of whether he was concerned with Practice for Classroom Teaching or Teaching Concept Development. The tutor's approach was both stable and characteristic and could be taken to be one of the major influences defining students' experiences of microteaching.

A COMPARISON OF APPROACHES

Tutors were grouped according to their declared aims and the MRCIAS data from their review conferences were combined to give composite pictures of these approaches to microteaching. This was done separately for the Year 1 and 2 studies and also for the two occasions within each year so that any differences could be identified. In fact the descriptions obtained were very consistent from occasion to occasion and from year to year. The overall descriptions obtained by combining all Year 1 data are now compared as illustrations of the findings. Any noticeable trends from occasion to occasion and differences from year to year are mentioned where relevant.

PCT and TCD comparisons

(a) Discussion content While PCT tutored groups on average devoted 22% of their conversations to the subject matter of the lessons, TCD tutored groups on average limited such discussion to less than 4% of all talk. Almost 50% of the TCD tutored groups' conversations were classified as general teaching skills (other than the weekly skill) as compared to 25% for the PCT tutored groups. PCT tutored groups gave attention to the weekly skill in only 3% of talk and the TCD groups even less at 1%. PCT groups devoted 18% of talk to the pupils and their management, whereas TCD groups focused 25% of talk on these themes. It was the PCT groups that felt the more obliged to talk about the microteaching system, though TCD groups did discuss it (PCT, 11%; TCD, 7%).

(b) Problem solving There were distinctive differences in the problem solving nature of the discussions in PCT and TCD tutored groups as evidenced by a comparison of the problem solving indices derived from the interaction matrices.

	PCT	TCD
Tutor Information Statement Ratio	0.50	0.89
Tutor Information Question Ratio	0.73	0.18

Almost 90% of the TCD tutors' exposition was concerned with supplying task-orientated information about teaching, compared to the 50% figure for the PCT tutors. Less than 20% of the TCD tutors' questioning behaviour involved requests for information, such as "What was the subject of your lesson? What aids did you use?" These lower level questions formed the major part of the questioning behaviour of the PCT tutors (73%). PCT tutors were found to increase the proportion of information seeking questions from the review of Lesson 3/4 to the review of Lesson 6/7 from 69% to 80% of their total questions. TCD, IIA tutors' information questions remained fairly steady at around 20%, while TCD, IIB tutors had reduced their use of information questions after the three week period from 23% to 12% of total questions.

	PCT	TCD
Tutor Analysis Statement Ratio	0.25	0.07
Tutor Analysis Question Ratio	0.24	0.78

These two indices are important in describing the differences between the indirect/direct strategies of the PCT and TCD tutors. 25% of the PCT tutors' exposition was concerned with giving evaluations of the students' lessons, compared with the 7% figure for the TCD tutors. Almost 80% of the TCD tutors' questioning behaviour was concerned with getting their students to analyse teaching, compared to the 24% figure for the PCT tutors. Also, the impressions gained from listening to the audiotapes would suggest that there were distinctive differences in the type of analytical questioning behaviour undertaken by the tutors. TCD tutors probed much deeper than PCT tutors in their pursuit of student self-analysis. They moved beyond the level of "How do you feel about it now that you have viewed the lesson?" to "Why?" questions interwoven with excerpts from the tutor's knowledge and experience of teaching (see Tutor Information Statement Ratios). PCT tutors had reduced their analysis questions by about 10% after the three week period, whereas IIA tutors had maintained their level of analytical questioning (76%) and IIB tutors had actually increased their analytical probing from

Descriptions of microteaching supervision

65% to 88% of total questioning.

	PCT	TCD
Tutor Suggestion Statement Ratio	0.24	0.04
Tutor Suggestion Question Ratio	0.03	0.05

The Tutor Suggestion Statement Ratio refers to the extent of tutor exposition that was concerned with direct advice. Note the difference in this index to the Tutor Information Statement Ratio. The former is associated with highly specific suggestions for change in approach. The latter is concerned with introducing additional information to help in the analysis of particular issues that have arisen in the discussion. 24% of the PCT tutors' exposition involved giving advice, compared to 4% for the TCD tutors. The proportion of the tutors' questioning behaviours asking students to proffer alternatives averaged around 4% for both PCT and TCD tutors.

(c) Interaction style The PCT and TCD tutor-led review discussions could also be characterised by the interaction strategies which were favoured. These strategies were summarised by the interaction indices.

	PDT	TCD
Tutor Talk Ratio	0.57	0.65

There was a consistent and stable difference of around 10% more tutor talk from TCD tutors than PCT tutors. At first sight this appears to be a surprising result, considering the TCD tutors' objectives of helping students to develop a personal understanding of teaching by a strategy of beginning from the students' own experiences of lessons they have taught. It appeared that a most important issue for investigation was the kind of tutor talk involved. Did the 10% difference apply to all types of tutor talk, or were there specific aspects of the TCD tutors' approaches that caused the differences in the overall amount of tutor talk? The other interaction indices help answer this question. The relative percentage of tutor talk differed little between the reviews of Lesson 3/4 and Lesson 6/7 for both the PCT and TCD tutors.

Descriptions of microteaching supervision

	PCT	TCD
The Tutor Statement Ratio	0.80	0.70

On average there was about 10% more tutor talk which was direct exposition from PCT tutors than from TCD tutors. The amount of tutor exposition remained fairly stable from the reviews of Lesson 3/4 to 6/7 for both PCT and TCD tutors.

	PCT	TCD
Tutor Questioning Ratio	0.10	0.11

On average about 10% of all tutor talk was questioning. Although there was no difference between PCT and TCD tutors in terms of total questioning, there were distinct differences in the type of question that were used, as has already been discussed in considering their use of problem solving.

	PCT	TCD
Tutor Extended Talk Ratio	0.65	0.62

This ratio indicated the extent of continuous tutor talk and showed little difference between tutors, or from occasion to occasion.

	PCT	TCD
Tutor Indirect/Direct Ratio	0.25	0.43

This ratio described the supervisor-supervisee relationship in terms of invitations to students to offer their opinions. TCD tutors adopted a much more indirect approach to their supervision than did PCT tutors.

	PCT	TCD
Tutor Response Ratio	0.08	0.19
Tutor Acceptance-Response Ratio	0.33	0.73

These indices indicate important and distinctive differences in the strategies adopted by the two groups of tutors. They summarise those tutor behaviours which prompt and encourage students to contribute to the review conference discussions. While the former ratio expresses such tutor acceptance remarks as a fraction of the total tutor

talk, the latter ratio, possibly a more sensitive
indicator, expresses tutor acceptance as a fraction
of the total tutor utterances which follow student
talk. 19% of all TCD tutor talk consisted of
accepting remarks whereas only 8% of all PCT tutor
talk consisted of tutor acceptance and these
percentages remained fairly stable over the three
week period. The Tutor Acceptance/Response Ratios
revealed that, for TCD tutors, 73% of tutor talk
which followed student talk was very supportive of
the students as compared to 33% for the PCT tutors.
Such results were consistent with the Tutor Analysis
Question Ratios. In the course of asking students
the 'Why?' questions required in analysis the TCD
tutors, in particular, were observed to be
continually prompting, encouraging and inviting
students to continue talking and thinking about
their teaching.

	PCT	TCD
Student Talk Ratio	0.41	0.34
Student Extended Talk Ratio	0.60	0.45
Student-Student Interaction Ratio	0.07	0.19

These indices provided an interesting contrast
in approaches. The Student Talk Ratio indicated
that on average students talked more in conferences
supervised by PCT tutors than in those supervised by
TCD tutors. However, when placing this index
alongside the very high Tutor Information Question
Ratio for PCT tutors and the high percentage (22%)
of the total PCT group discussion that was concerned
with lesson content (compared to 3% for TCD
supervised conferences), it would seem likely that
much of the student talk in PCT groups consisted of
telling the tutor about what they had taught in
their lessons. This inference was confirmed by
listening to the review conference audiotapes and
checking the notes taken in the field diary.
The Student Extended Talk Ratio measured the
proportion of continuous inter-student talk and
averaged higher for the PCT tutored groups than the
TCD tutored groups. This index was developed in the
hope that it would highlight a tutor approach which
encouraged a student to elaborate upon his own ideas
and feelings at length. In fact this did not happen
as expected for TCD tutors. The Tutor Response
Ratios and the Tutor Acceptance/Response Ratios have
indicated that the TCD tutors very frequently
interjected short reinforcing comments, e.g. "Yes",

"Go on", etc., into the flow of student talk in order to keep the student talking.

However, the Student-Student Interaction Ratio was higher for the TCD supervised conferences than the PCT supervised conferences, indicating more student to student verbal interaction without tutor involvement. This indicated a supervisory approach that was less tutor centred and that valued and promoted inter-student discussion. While the proportion of student-student interaction remained fairly stable after the three week period in PCT tutored groups, in the case of TCD tutored groups student-student interaction increased after the three week period when the students had acquired more experience of the supervisor and the microteaching process and possibly had developed more confidence in their own views.

IA and IB comparisons
(a) Discussion content As expected from the tutors' aims classification, groups with a IA (Problem Solving for Teaching Skills) tutor talked much more about the weekly skill than did groups with a IB (Problem Solving for Teaching Practice) tutor. Surprisingly perhaps, the weekly skill was not discussed as much as may have been expected - 8% for IA groups; 1% for IB groups; 2% for all groups). Over the three week period there was an increased focus on lesson content from 14% to 31% for IB groups at the 'expense' of talk about teacher behaviour which was reduced from 34% to 21%. This was consistent with the IB tutors' predominant aim of preparing students for their block teaching practice and their first teaching appointment. The emphasis was being firmly placed on the ability to teach a 'good' lesson. In contrast, the discussion content pattern of the IA supervised groups remained fairly stable.

(b) Problem solving IA and IB tutored groups were found to be very similar in terms of their problem solving behaviours which remained very stable from occasion to occasion, as indicated by the problem solving indices.

(c) Interaction style The interaction indices of IA and IB tutored groups were also very similar and stable from occasion to occasion.

IIA and IIB comparisons
(a) Discussion content The emphasis on general
teaching skills was high for both the IIA (TCD -
learning experiences) and IIB (TCD - relationships)
tutored groups. IIA groups increased their
consideration of teaching skills issues from 46% of
all talk on Occasion 1 to 60% on Occasion 2, whereas
IIB groups increased slightly from 45% to 48%. The
IIA groups talked more about the lesson (15%) than
did the IIB groups (6%) as expected from the aims
categorisation.

Groups tutored by IIB supervisors were much
more concerned with pupil behaviour and classroom
management (33%) than groups tutored by IIA
supervisors (12%). Such group discussion was
consistent with the IIB supervisors' aims
emphasising an understanding of children, and the
relationship of the student as teacher with the
pupils. The IIB groups increased the proportion of
talk concerning pupils from 28% to 38% over the 3
week period. IIA tutored groups, however, decreased
their focus on the pupils over this period from 19%
to 5%.

(b) Problem solving IIA and IIB tutored groups were
very similar indeed in their problem solving
characteristics. The only noticeable differences
were in the amount of tutor information statements
(IIA, 83% of tutor exposition talk; IIB, 93%) and
tutor analysis statements (IIA, 13%; IIB, 3%). IIA
tutors increased their information statements from
77% of tutor talk on Occasion 1 to 93% on Occasion 2
and IIB tutors also increased their analysis
statements slightly from 90% to 95%. IIB tutors
gave about 3% of total exposition on analysis on
both occasions, but IIA tutors reduced their giving
of analysis from 18% in the review of Lesson 3/4 to
5% in review of Lesson 6/7.

(c) Interaction style IIA and IIB groups were also
similar in interaction style and both were
consistent from occasion to occasion. The IIB
tutors were rather more indirect in style than the
IIA tutors (indirect/direct ratios: IIA, 0.39; IIB,
0.46) and also more supportive of student responses
(acceptance/response ratios: IIA, 0.69; IIB, 0.76).

CONCLUSIONS

Overall the approaches of PCT and TCD tutors were
clearly distinguishable, but those of the IA and IB
tutors and of the IIA and IIB tutors differed only
in a few respects. The PCT tutored groups focused
on the discussion of general teaching skills and on
the lesson, whereas the TCD groups focused even more
on the general teaching skills and also on the
pupils and their relationships with the student
teacher.
    PCT and TCD tutors employed very different
general patterns in their problem solving behaviour.
TCD tutors were almost totally concerned in their
exposition with task-orientated statements about
teaching (89%), with only a little talk expressing
evaluation (7%), and even less containing offers of
advice or suggestion for improvement (4%). PCT
tutors, on the other hand, devoted about one quarter
of their exposition to telling students the
strengths and weaknesses of their lesson, with
another quarter of the tutor statements providing
specific suggestions for improvement. The other 50%
of PCT tutor exposition was providing information
about teaching.
    About three quarters of the PCT tutors'
questions were asking for information, whereas only
about one fifth of the TCD tutors' questioning
behaviour was information-seeking. The TCD tutors
devoted about three quarters of their questions to
promoting student analysis whereas the PCT tutors
employed only about one quarter of their questions'
for this purpose. Questions requiring students to
offer alternatives (i.e. 'how they might teach it
differently now that they had viewed and discussed
their lessons') occurred very infrequently - for
both PCT and TCD tutors only about one twentieth of
their questioning was directed at this task.
    In terms of their interaction style TCD tutors
involved their students more in collaborative
discussion than did PCT tutors. The Tutor Response
Ratios and the Tutor Acceptance-Response Ratios were
considerably higher for the TCD tutors than for the
PCT tutors. This was confirmed by listening to the
many recordings of review conferences in which there
was much encouragement and reinforcement being shown
by the TCD tutors who were continually orientating
the students into a deeper analysis of teaching.
The illuminative research evidence revealed that the
tone of the TCD tutors' approach was one of genuine
interest, framed in a manner that valued the

development of the student's own experiences and opinions and that regarded this development as being of central importance in microteaching. The illuminative research also confirmed the finding of the Tutor Analysis Question Ratios that the quality of student talk was more analytical in the TCD tutored groups than in the PCT tutored groups.

Thus the differences in supervisory aims were reflected in tutors' conference behaviours, as described by MRCIAS. Students' reactions to their supervision also provided interesting contrasts. The views of students about the approaches adopted by their tutors are reported in Chapters Six and Seven.

Chapter 6.

TUTOR-STUDENT INTERPERSONAL RELATIONSHIPS

There were a number of threads in this whole
research programme which had pointed to the
affective relationships between tutor and students
in the review conference as being worthy of close
examination in the case study. The preliminary
exploratory investigations had suggested that
students were learning many things in microteaching
besides teaching skills, in particular, they were
exploring their relationships with children and
their own feelings and attitudes about becoming a
teacher. This had led to the development of
research instruments for measuring students' and
tutors' perceptions of interpersonal relationships
in review conferences. The literature survey on
supervision in teacher education had focused
attention on Dussault's theory of supervision as
teaching, with the affective meaning in the
supervisor-student discussions being of particular
importance. The interviews with tutors about their
aims had revealed the high value that all tutors
placed on developing good interpersonal
relationships with their students. This was
especially so for Teaching Concept Development
tutors who sought an affective atmosphere in their
review conferences that would sensitise students to
the importance of the affective domain in the
dynamics of teaching and learning.
    The case study followed a number of paths in
investigating the interpersonal relationships
between tutors and their students. The systematic
observation provided descriptions of supervisory
strategies which promoted affective learning.
Student and tutor perceptions of interpersonal
relationships were measured. Interviews with
students and tutors provided opportunities to ask
about the affective meaning in the review

conferences and its part in the process of learning to be a teacher.

INTERACTION STYLE AND AFFECTIVE MEANING

The Teaching Concept Development (TCD) tutors had said they valued affective aims in their approach to microteaching and the TCD - Relationships Orientated (IIB) tutors were especially desirous of promoting affective learning in the review conferences. The descriptions of review conference strategies reported in Chapter 5 have indicated that these tutors did use an approach which was distinctive and which contained a set of tutor verbal behaviours which were intended to build interpersonal relationships.

Blumberg (1970) had found that indirect verbal behaviours by a supervisor were interpreted by his student in terms of personal consideration. The indirect/direct nature of the review conference discussions was taken as the summary characteristic which indicated the extent to which tutors worked to provide the supportive atmosphere which would draw out their students. The case study has revealed that TCD tutors did use a more indirect style than did Practice for Classroom Teaching (PCT) tutors and that the prominent features of this indirect style were the tutors' questioning and responding behaviours. TCD tutors used somewhat less 'telling' behaviour than PCT tutors and, although both groups of tutors used questioning behaviour to the same extent, there were considerable differences in the types and purposes of these questions. PCT tutors favoured closed questions which asked for recall of information whereas TCD tutors' questions were more open-ended and more penetrating in that students were asked to think analytically. PCT tutors' questions often focused on the lesson content and structure whereas TCD tutors frequently asked about the student as a person, inviting them to talk about their feelings, values and opinions. These types of question were in keeping with the tutors' aims. The PCT tutors had short term aims, helping their students teach 'good' lessons as a preparation for block teaching practice in school. The TCD tutors had long term aims, encouraging students to build their own understanding of teaching.

TCD tutors made very considerable use of responding behaviours, working hard to convey their genuine interest and supportive attitude. Very

frequent reinforcement was provided to encourage
students to think out loud and form their own
concepts and values. Through their use of accepting
behaviours and reinforcing comments TCD tutors were
indicating that students' contributions were wanted,
respected, valued and necessary. This could be the
reason for the observed difference in the patterns
of talk in the groups. In PCT groups almost all the
conversations were from and to the tutor, whereas in
TCD group discussions there were some
student-student interactions which did not involve
the tutor. Also, the extent of these
student-student interactions increased over the
three week period between observations.

TCD tutors were certainly providing the
opportunities for affective learning in the review
conferences and, if supervision is regarded as
teaching, this should also help students learn about
the affective dimension of their own teaching. Were
the students perceptive of these opportunities?
Were they becoming sensitive to the importance of
affective relationships in the dynamics of teaching
and learning? This first question is now explored
and the second will be taken up in the next chapter.

PERCEPTIONS OF INTERPERSONAL RELATIONSHIPS

Students' perceptions
The 144 students in the Year 1 study had been
invited to respond to the Student Relationship
Inventory (SRI) on each of the two data collecting
occasions. SRI asked students about their
relationships with their tutors. 136 students (94%)
responded to the first administration (SRI1) and 119
(83%) to the second administration (SRI2) three
weeks later. The means and standard deviations of
the SRI scores for all students and for students
grouped by the aims classification of their tutors
are reported in Table 6.1.

There was little change in overall scores from
occasion to occasion though all groups did show a
slight increase from Occasion 1 to 2. A one-way
analysis of variance found no significant difference
between these groups for both SRI1 and SRI2 scores.
The differences in students' perceptions were not
distinctive enough to merit classification in terms
of their tutors' aims categories. The SRI mean
scores for students supervised by TCD tutors were
higher than for students supervised by PCT tutors
and the standard deviations were lower for students

94

Table 6.1: Students' perceptions of their supervisor

Student groups	SRI1 Mean	S.D.	SRI2 Mean	S.D.
All students	191	34	199	41
IA tutored students	182	34	187	41
IB tutored students	189	30	193	31
IIA tutored students	192	25	202	29
IIB tutored students	194	21	200	26

supervised by TCD tutors.

Students had been supervised in groups of four in the review conferences. What agreement existed among the students in each group in terms of their SRI scores? Were the SRI scores a characteristic of the individual students or of the groups, and hence of the tutors? A one way analysis of variance was applied to the 38 groups of students' SRI scores. The between group variance was significantly greater than the within group variance ($p < 0.05$) in the case of SRI1 scores but did not quite reach significance level for SRI2 scores. Thus there was some evidence that students in a group shared a fairly common view of the relationship with their tutor, and that the opinions of the different groups were comparatively widely dispersed. These trends would suggest, tentatively, that the SRI scores were indicative of a tutor characteristic.

Within a week of responding to SRI the students had also responded to the Self-Concept as Teacher Scale (SCATS) which measured their opinions as to the contribution that microteaching was making to their development as teachers. 140 students (97%) responded to the first administration (SCATS1) and 131 (91%) to the second administration (SCATS2). There were no differences found between the SCATS1 and SCATS2 mean total scores and mean sub-scale scores. A one way analysis of variance was used to see if there were any significant differences between the scores of students grouped by their teacher's aims classification (IA, IB, IIA, IIB). The supervisor sub-scale was the only sub-scale for which the between groups variance was significantly

greater ($p<0.05$) than the within group variance.
Students grouped by their tutors' common aims saw
their supervisors similarly in terms of the extent
to which they helped them develop as teachers.
Another one way analysis of variance was carried out
to see if students in the same review group had
similar views about their development through
microteaching. The between group variance for the
38 groups of students was found to be significantly
greater than the within group variance for the
competence ($p<0.05$), supervision ($p<0.01$) and peer
group ($p<0.05$) sub-scales scores for both SCATS1 and
SCATS2. Students in the same review group felt
similarly about the helpfulness of their supervisors
and peer groups and about their own growing
competence as teachers.

Overall the findings of these measurement
studies suggested that the students in the same
review group had similar views about their
relationships with their tutors and about the extent
to which the supervision that they experienced was
helpful. There were no significant differences
between students grouped by their tutors' common
aims in terms of their views of their relationships
with their tutors, but these groups did differ
significantly in their regard for the helpfulness of
their supervision. There were no noticeable changes
over the three week period between measurements.

The students' perceptions were also obtained in
the student interviews. The following brief
vignettes are presented as representative
illustrations of the views of the sample of students
interviewed. The names are fictitious.

Vignette 1
Mark was in a review group supervised by Mr. Smith
whose aims had been classified as PCT, IA. Mark's
frustration was clear. He had experienced the
review conference as being entirely controlled by
the tutor, who was perceived to have an
unnecessarily negative approach. Tutor evaluation
and assessment dominated much of Mark's thinking.
Yet despite the criticism of his supervisor, he
expressed positive attitudes towards the teaching
experiences provided in microteaching and he valued
the opportunity to view the videorecording.

"It's just that Mr. Smith looks at the lesson of you
at face value. That's the lesson and this is how it
came over, not how you felt... or how you think the
children felt... or how the lessons differ... You

just go in and teach and come out... He has a certain view and, as far as I can see, he just sticks to it... It's not that he talks a lot about the skill. He doesn't. It's just that I think that he expects to see that we have planned for the skill... What he does is that he looks at the lesson and picks out any places where he thinks that we're doing it wrong... Assessment is at the back of your mind all the time... There's not much you can do about it."

Vignette 2
Jane was supervised by Dr. George (PCT, IB aims). The focus that she brought to the review conference was one of satisfaction that she "has got a lot done" in her lesson, combined with a concern that she had perhaps tried to cover too much material. The interview revealed that although she did make clear her concerns to her supervisor, he did not take these issues up for discussion, choosing instead to point out the obvious faults.

"He told me what I knew already sort of thing... Yet last week, if you had asked me, I would have said that he should have given us constructive criticism... Whenever he started to give it I didn't like it that much... He didn't have a conversation. He just said points that were wrong, but I had known them wrong and I just felt rotten about the lesson then, and therefore I got very defensive and clammed up. I think actually if he had given me some support rather than criticism it would have been better because I knew where I was wrong... I knew what I did... I felt that I was going to have to work on my lesson plan a bit more. He has a bit more experience, yes. But it is supposed to be a two-way thing, or so I felt... There's not much point, unless we are going to have a lecture. You should be able to talk. There should be a conversation set up, and not just a one-way process. Two people talking at each other rather than to each other - if that happens you get defensive. It's very confusing. When he said nothing but good points it was worthless, and now when he says nothing but bad points it's worse... I wonder if other groups are having this problem."

The supervisory approach of switching from support to criticism was an issue of concern common to all the PCT (IA and IB) tutored students that were interviewed. These students saw their supervisors as allowing only a week or two for 'support' before switching to 'criticism'. The sudden change in tutor strategy experienced by the students appeared to be totally unexpected. Some students like Jane expressed frustration and anger. Others simply accepted the strategy as 'the way it was done':

"You are taking note of what he likes and dislikes. There's a lot of feelings go unsaid, I think... You just accept him... If he feels that way, O.K... You've got to try and adopt the approach that he wants, because after all he's going to be marking it in the end... So there is no use me holding on to the approach I think is right. You do go into your lesson to enjoy it, but the sessions afterwards are certainly not very open... There's just not the time. I do enjoy the microteaching... You know yourself where your bad points and good points are, so you begin to question the value of some of these reviewing sessions." (Brian, IB tutored student)

Vignette 3
Janet was supervised by Mr. Foster, whose aims had been classified as TCD, IIA. Unlike Mark and Jane, Janet stressed the communicative nature of the review conference, together with a very positive attitude towards the approach adopted by her supervisor. One interesting aspect of microteaching specifically identified by three other students as well as Janet was the unusual exposure felt by students undertaking microteaching. Janet was also able to relate the teaching skills introduced in lectures to her practical experiences of the microlessons and review conferences.

"I feel that the discussion was very worthwhile... I knew when I was teaching that it was a bit above their heads, but the discussion did help a lot... and not just me... I think the others in the group learned by it too. We do a fair bit of talking between the four of us... A point would come up... and we would give our reasons for doing it a certain way... Then we would think up alternative ways and reasons... and of course Mr. Foster would add to it alternatives that we perhaps never thought of. So it's very practical, in a funny kind of way. There's no tension really... Behind it all the time you know that he's a lecturer, but it's not an overbearing sort of thing. He asks a lot of what you might call higher order questions, to coin a

phrase... Yes he likes to make you think about it
for yourself. There's something about this
microteaching... You could feel very exposed... It's
so searching... It makes it a lot easier if you do
like him... I find him O.K. He seems - I'm talking
about the lectures now - he seems to want us to
practise a skill each week. We don't... The
lectures help in another kind of way... They help
you to think about what you are going to do whenever
you go into the room... They help you to talk about
what you have done... or how you could have done it
differently. It strikes me that there's a lot to
this microteaching. It's very concentrated and you
learn very quickly. It's very different from
anything I have ever done before."

Vignette 4
Bill was supervised by Dr. Wilson, a TCD, IIB tutor.
Like Janet, Bill emphasised the student-orientated
nature of the review conference and the control that
the group experienced over what was actually
discussed. As with all the TCD tutored students
that were interviewed, very positive attitudes were
expressed as to the supervisor's intentions and
behaviour.

"He lets you speak first and then he'll maybe offer
some opinion or some point... You develop it from
there for yourself. I don't think the tutor is
telling you as such... he's maybe offering you
advice, but he's not laying out to you what or the
way you have to do it. It's a very open-ended
approach... He's putting everybody at ease... He's
not deliberately putting anybody on the spot. It's
hard to explain... lots of ideas come up in the
conversation... He never says, 'You must do this' or
'That is the wrong way to do it'... You learn an
awful lot just because he's there. He stimulates
ideas in your mind... and brings in a lot more
ideas... different ways of looking at some part of
teaching... and he's bringing out comparisons in the
way we feel about things... or the way we are doing
certain things with the children... not just about
how we are teaching, but about how we are reacting
to the children... He's really great... He seems to
have a great understanding of teaching... He gets
you to think. That's it... and yet he's very
practical. You're really exhausted after the two
hour sessions. He really gets you thinking.
Somehow he seems... aware... that you are feeling
your way... I've learned a lot during the past few

weeks."

Tutors' perceptions

Two Tutor Relationship Inventories were developed
out of the already established Student Relationship
Inventory. The first, TRIA, (where A refers to
'aims') was administered prior to supervised
microteaching and asked all tutors to describe
themselves in terms of the kind of relationship that
they hoped to achieve with their students. The
second, TRIE, (where E refers to the relationship
'experienced') was administered during the seventh
week of microteaching at the end of the data
collecting phase of the Year 1 study and asked all
tutors to describe themselves in terms of the
relationship that actually existed with their
students. TRIA and TRIE were regarded as the most
tentative of measures since this was their first
application to a relatively small number of tutors.

Tutors were grouped according to their aims
classification and one way analyses of variance were
carried out on the separate TRIA and TRIE scores to
see if tutors with common aims both sought and
experienced similar relationships with their
students. The between group variance was
significantly greater than the within group variance
for the TRIE scores ($p<0.01$) but no significant
difference was found in the case of the TRIA scores.
The creation of TRIE had required only minor
modifications to SRI, but major changes were
required to construct TRIA. Many of the items had
to be altered substantially and even be reversed
from negative to positive form in order to be
meaningful. Even then tutors reported difficulty in
interpreting TRIA items. Thus TRIA was not really
established as a valid instrument.

Correlation of TRIE and SRI2 scores yielded a
Pearson product moment correlation coefficient of
0.33 which gave a significant t value (d.f.=32,
$p<0.05$). This small but significant correlation
suggested, very tentatively, a relationship between
tutors' experiences of working with their students
and students' experiences of working with their
tutors.

At the end of the Year 2 investigations (see
Chapter Four) the 8 tutors in the stratified random
sample were interviewed to obtain their reactions to
the researcher's findings with regard to their
supervision. The following comments are
representative of the tutors' attitudes concerning
the relationship with their students.

Tutor-student interpersonal relationships

PCT tutors
"I think microteaching is critically dependent on
the students being mature enough to accept
criticism, which I don't think in many cases they
are. I mean, as students, they are not aware of
their mistakes, either as a result of seeing them,
or hearing them, or as a result of my gentle hints
during our discussion... And if that happens there
is no benefit from microteaching. They are not
going to profit... I think that is where the biggest
weakness is, and it is a weakness which I am saying
that they don't take kindly to being pointed out. I
often also try to encourage the other students to
criticise each other in a constructive fashion, but
that never happens. So it results basically in me
saying what I felt was wrong. Then, usually, they
politely acknowledge it without sometimes really
believing it I think... and it really is all a bit
stilted. They are afraid that the others will
criticise them, and it goes back to this sort of
inferiority complex, sensitivity about themselves,
not wanting to expose themselves and their
weaknesses... not wanting to admit weaknesses. No,
they prefer to play safe and just leave any
criticism to me."

"I don't go into conferences saying to myself, 'They
must like me. They must love me.' I suppose if
people show they participate and they have a certain
respect for me... maybe this satisfies me and my
image of myself as a teacher in a university
setting."

"I believe that I know what's best for these
inexperienced students... My experience tells me the
things that they need to hear. Whether they like me
or dislike me is... somehow... irrelevant!"

"I suspect our job is not to be 'liked'. I would
hope that it would be 'to be respected'."

TCD tutors
"They have opinions about the lessons. They know
whether they are satisfied with it or not...
Sometimes they can't put their finger on why, but
they certainly know if the gut reaction to it has
been good or bad... so part of our viewing is to try
and do that for them, and therefore bring a purpose
to the viewing. It's building on their experiences,
their impressions, their observations, their
feelings. I try not to tell them what my opinion is

because that gives them the opportunity of taking it or leaving it. I am trying to almost force them, or 'challenge' them is a better word, to produce their own thought out evaluations, and also to do it for each other."

"There is a symbol in a sense of the all-powerful parent arriving... So there is an enormous tension that has to be got over for them to start looking at the lesson realistically... What the powerful parent has to do is to validate, and say that you are O.K., but at another level to demolish the myth by saying that you can now validate yourself. 'You have got to get into that business. You don't have to rely on me to tell you that you are a good teacher; you have to do that for yourself!' Some of the questions that we are trying to get at here are of such a tremendously threatening kind that you have to almost experience the threat yourself. In order for them to answer, you must provide them with some kind of support and resource."

EXCERPTS FROM THE REVIEW CONFERENCES

The following excerpts are presented in order to familiarise the reader with the range of tutors' approaches to the review conferences. It is hoped that the excerpts will help the reader flesh out the descriptions that have been discussed in this chapter and the previous one, especially with regard to the interactive style used and the interpersonal relationships created and maintained. Excerpts displaying extremes in tutors' strategies have been avoided as misrepresentative of the complex reality of microteaching supervision. The names are fictitious.

Excerpt 1
Excerpt 1 was drawn from a Lesson 4 review conference, supervised by a IA tutor who had a definite leaning towards a IB approach. He was concerned that students appreciated the link with the lecture programme of weekly skills and he used the relevant skill schedule to rate the students' lessons. The discussion was restricted to a review of the specific lesson, and was typical of a Practice for Classroom Teaching Approach to the supervision of microteaching.

TUTOR Well let's move on then. John, what were you doing?
JOHN Well this week I was trying to keep it more simple. The objective was simply for the children to know that when metals are heated they will expand. It was fairly simple.
TUTOR Well let's jump in and see.
(John's lesson is viewed on the videotape.)
TUTOR That's interesting compared with last week, isn't it? What were you aware of in the differences - well, you were trying to make it different, weren't you?
JOHN Really simplifying it.
TUTOR Simplifying it, yes.
JOHN Trying to avoid complicating it if I could.
TUTOR Well, did you feel that was a step that was justified?
JOHN Oh I did, the child was able to discuss it.
TUTOR No, sorry. I was thinking of your tactic of trying to keep it as simple as possible - simplifying the ideas. Is there anything you could have done to avoid recapping on the previous week? Is there anything that you could have done maybe to extend... maybe some application of the term "expansion".
JOHN I was tempted to, but I think the time is a problem. I was going to bring in a selection of metals. I was going to bring in something else to give an example, but I don't think the time would fit it.
TUTOR One thing that I was sensing as a difficulty, was avoiding using the terms "physical and chemical changes", and you were talking about heating and combustion... and burning... and you chose not to use them, which was probably right. But that left you with a bit of a problem as to how to do it or what word to use, what verb to use. In the simplification of language there is a point that you get to where you can't really be much simpler.
JOHN I meant to say that the metal ball was copper, but actually it was brass, and they could see that it wasn't copper.
TUTOR Yes.
JOHN Calling it copper or brass, and trying to explain what brass is. I found that I was having difficulty trying to explain what brass is.
TUTOR Yes. Now the theme was teacher liveliness this week, am I right?
JOHN Yes.
TUTOR You reckoned you were lively?
JOHN I could have been livelier. It didn't seem

the sort of experiment that would lend itself to
liveliness anyhow.
HELEN   Well you did move about, and you did gesture,
you know. You used gestures. I think if you are
moving about, you are lively.
CAROL   I think if you keep away from the desk and
the board it helps. It's hard to get out from
behind the desk. You sort of have to walk round it.
TUTOR   It's just that one doesn't realise this.
Once or twice in the past we took videotapes of
students as examples of different styles of
teaching. Until you see these side by side in
succession, say five minutes of this style followed
by five minutes of that, one doesn't realise the
enormous difference there can be. I wouldn't
imagine that you would wish to be more animated.
CAROL   The voice, I think that helps. I tend to
stay too high. You vary the speed at which you
speak or pause more. When you ask a question, that
you give them time to think. That all helps to give
you variation.
JOHN   It's very difficult.
CAROL   I know it is, but you have to be patient and
let them think.
JOHN   Especially when one of the children starts
talking about something else.
HELEN   Yes they can sidetrack you and you don't want
to say, 'Shut up'.
JOHN   You get thrown off your guard very easily.
TUTOR   I know. It takes time to know when to do
anything, to sense to do anything at all, except
ignore. Well you have these schedules to rate
yourself. It's quite useful, I think, to have a go
at this, even if you feel that you are not that
confident to alter or change your approach. Maybe
it's an accumulative affect, looking at these
various skills week by week, and gradually you
become more and more aware of all that goes into
this rather complex art of teaching.
(After allowing time for the students to complete
the rating scales with reference to John's lesson,
the tutor led the group through the schedule, point
by point. What was evident from the tutor's remarks
was that he was using the scales subtly to tell the
students just what he regarded as a good teaching
performance.)

Excerpt 2
Excerpt 2 was drawn from the third review conference
of a IB tutored group, and provided an example of a
Practice for Classroom Teaching supervisor's

approach. The discussion was straight-forward in
style and was restricted to consideration of Anne's
lesson. There were few opportunities provided to
widen the issues under discussion. IA and IB tutors
rarely used the review experience to probe for a
wider understanding of teaching or of students'
personal feelings. Even at this fairly early stage
of reviewing students' lessons the prescriptive
tendencies of the tutor were evident in defining
what he regarded as a good performance. In fact
this excerpt was rather less prescriptive than most.
Advice was given by the tutor as expert.

TUTOR   What was your lesson about this week, Anne?
ANNE   I did Transport and the difference between
Private and Public and Commercial ... buses as
opposed to cars - things like that.
TUTOR   So you were looking at Systems of Transport?
ANNE   Yea.
TUTOR   Let's have a look at the lesson, then. (Group
view the videotape of Anne's lesson.)
TUTOR   What were the questions?
ANNE   Name the three commercial vehicles and what
was the difference between Private and Public
transport? How did you travel to school this
morning? Was it by Public, Private, or Commercial
transport?
TUTOR   And what kind of answers did you get?
ANNE   The three girls were quite good, O.K. The
two boys didn't get it finished, they only got three
done.
TUTOR   Yes. Were they getting the right idea?
ANNE   Yes, but at the start they definitely weren't
at first.
TUTOR   Yes. That came across there. Yes they found
it difficult to categorise.
ANNE   Aha.
TUTOR   What did you make of the lesson yourself?
ANNE   I definitely don't think I planned it right,
especially 'vehicle', the word 'vehicle'. I didn't
clarify that at all really.
TUTOR   They took 'vehicle' to be a car when you did
ask the question.
ANNE   Yes.
TUTOR   And obviously it has a much wider context.
ANNE   Aha.
TUTOR   So you needed to slow it down.
ANNE   Yes.
TUTOR   I remember seeing once on the Portrush road,
someone had put up a sign and it reflected the
difficulty the roadmen had in spelling - they spelt

VECHILE - the roadmen couldn't cope. It's a difficult word.

ANNE   Aha.

TUTOR   It's really not one... They may have come across people using it but they wouldn't necessarily understand it.

ANNE   Yes.

TUTOR   Any other comments?

MARY   Maybe it was that they didn't understand the words like 'commercial' but she really kept them to the point when she did the three divisions sort of... She didn't... sort of... go on to anything else, which I thought was very good. She didn't... sort of try to expand on it. She just kept to...

TUTOR   So she focused on the point.

MARY   I think it was maybe just the words like 'commercial', but there was nothing else she could have used sort of, as a heading.

TUTOR   No.

MARY   Once she said 'vehicles carried goods' - things like lorries, things like that, they knew all right what it was. I think maybe it was just, sort of, the words that got them maybe, because she kept on the same lines all the time. They were very interested because she had them with her all the time. Whenever they were to give suggestions, and things like that, she had a reward and she went back to one, one of the ones didn't know it. She went back. She said, 'Do you understand now?' She tried to reinforce it.

TUTOR   So she had a clear idea of what she wanted to do, even though there were difficulties. She kept at it and she reinforced the learning through the picture and through the questions to try and communicate some level of understanding of these three categories.

MARY   Aha.

TUTOR   But it was hard going. Any other comments at all?

JOHN   Maybe it was more or less just the topic. I think if it had maybe been simpler - just to deal with the land and sea, maybe just concentrate on the different vehicles.

TUTOR   Yes.

JOHN   When she went on the Public, Private and Commercial they got a bit stuck.

TUTOR   Aha.

JOHN   Maybe three was a bit too much for her.

TUTOR   Yes especially with the words like 'commercial' - words they don't use. 'Public', even is a word maybe they don't use in their own

language, you know, in their own conversation.
ANNE   They seemed to think 'Private' was the
Queen's coach or something...
TUTOR Yes. So it's a good attempt at a difficult
subject but I think you need to watch really what
you pick, you know. It was a bit difficult. I
think this is true really generally of children of
the Primary School. To make the generalisation into
the category is a bit more difficult than we
imagine.
ANNE   Yes.
TUTOR Well anyway that was quite good. I think
once or twice you tended to be a wee bit theatrical,
you know the kind of sweeps of the hand.
ANNE   Yes.
TUTOR But maybe when you see yourself do it...
ANNE   I'm aware I do that because I do languages
and it colours the way I talk. I can't help it. I
think there's no harm but... I use my hands an awful
lot even when talking to normal people; it's not...
TUTOR Well that's alright... That's fair enough,
but I think you can see sometimes... you can see
yourself that it can become a bit exaggerated, you
know. I think it's good to use your hands and maybe
a teacher should use their hands and their body
more, but you need to be aware of how it can become
a bit comical if it is overdone.
ANNE   Yes.
TUTOR Do you know what I mean?
ANNE   Yes.
TUTOR So don't worry about it. I was just... but
try and control your sweeping gestures.
Right. Who was next?

Excerpt 3

This excerpt was taken from the conference of a IIA
tutor in the review of Lesson 3. The group had just
viewed the lesson of a student later described by
the tutor as "making a fairly weak start in
microteaching". Thus, it contained more stated
tutor analysis than usually found in a IIA approach.
Noteworthy features were the quality of the support
given by the tutor and the way in which he used the
other students' evaluations to establish the
progress this particular student had made since the
last lesson. Then, from a position of support, he
drew out of the student those aspects of his
teaching that required further thought and
development. Compared to the IA and IB examples
this conference provided more opportunities for

student opinions to be expressed and this was
achieved through the tutor's questioning and
reinforcement strategies. There was also a subtle
emphasis on general teaching behaviour and
understanding, characteristic of a TCD approach.
The IIA thrust was evident in the lesson plan and
structure being used as the enabling context in
which the teaching skills were embedded.

TUTOR Well, what about that now in terms of a
comparison of that with last week's, the
improvements you are looking for. Do you feel...?
NEIL   Well I really didn't see any difference at
all.
TUTOR Did you not notice any difference? What did
you notice, Vera?
VERA   I think it seems a lot better. Last week he
seemed nervous.
NEIL   Last week was terrible.
TUTOR Yes.
NEIL   But, it's my voice.
KEITH He still talks fairly quickly in some places.
NEIL   Yes.
TUTOR Can you identify why you think it is
better... What do you see different about this week?
VERA   It's much more natural and a lot more...
well... clearer.
JANET There's more expression.
TUTOR Yes, definitely, I think. There's a lot more
expression.
JANET Last week he just read a book.
TUTOR Now do you see where that was coming from?
How was your voice more expressive? We all feel
that about it this week.
NEIL   Because I was more... relating to the pupils.
TUTOR Well there's quite a number of reasons -
that's one of them.
KEITH He was more active.
TUTOR More active, exactly, yes, you were
definitely more active this week. This week's skill
is teacher liveliness, isn't that right?
NEIL   Yes.
TUTOR Well there's a lot more liveliness there
compared to what you had last week, and especially
to what you had a fortnight ago.
(Videotape adjusted to replay a section)
Now you see your voice has been used naturally
there. You're interested in what you're teaching
and you're active in what you're teaching. You're
not having to read it all off, you internalised it
and you are presenting it as explanation and it is a

much more natural situation... Hence your voice has
become quite naturally more expressive. You simply,
as it were... removed a lot of the strait jackets
that you were wearing.
NEIL   I think my voice is too low.
TUTOR   No, no, we're talking in terms of lack of
expression, lack of variety, lack of interest.
That's what we were talking about last week. But
this week you have made a big step forward in terms
of definitely having it... and notice another thing.
 It's not just coming from your voice. Do you see
it there in your facial expression as well? Did you
notice that? You are smiling at times...
NEIL   Mm?
TUTOR   You had an enjoyable experience there.
NEIL   Yes. I think so.
TUTOR   You see... last week you were knotted up
tight. Here, you were using your face nicely. You
were showing your interest in the pupils... You were
showing your interest in the subject. You were
prepared to share a joke with them when the
opportunity arose. You laughed and they laughed,
you know what I mean.
NEIL   Yes.
TUTOR   You see what I mean now. Your whole manner
allowed your voice to be more expressive.
NEIL   Yes.
TUTOR   And it just wasn't the voice on its own, look
at the gestures. How do you compare your gestures
this week with last week?
NEIL   Well, actually, I seem to be moving around
more this week.
TUTOR   And there you see... you have a lot of
gestures with your arms and your body position...
you moved about a lot and you went down to
individuals and you walked back and forward. You
know what I mean. So those things all go together,
an aspect of interest and liveliness. Well there is
another thing now you see, another interesting thing
that ties up with this. You feel that you've been
like that because you had more confidence in what
you were teaching.
NEIL   Yes, that's true.
TUTOR   And you had a lot more confidence in your
material this week and that's another thing.
NEIL   Yes, I had good material this week.
TUTOR   Exactly, and you felt better prepared?
NEIL   Yes.
TUTOR   Yes, well now ...
NEIL   I felt I could handle it better this week.
TUTOR   Well if you learn that and never let go of

it, you have learned an awful lot about teaching.
Teaching's being natural to people... and you can't
be natural unless you feel relaxed, and you can't be
relaxed unless you feel confident... and you can't
be confident unless you know you are well prepared.
NEIL   Yes, I can see that.
TUTOR   The whole pattern of your lesson has
developed just like that. You felt that your
materials were better structured. You felt you were
better prepared... you had more confidence... you
didn't have to read your notes.
NEIL   No, I didn't use my notes.
TUTOR   The lesson content this time too was better
structured. Now you have a better idea of what it
means to teach a concept. I think you have a gain
there too.
NEIL   Yes.
TUTOR   So, you also felt more confident for that
reason.
NEIL   Aha.
TUTOR   Would you agree that your class would be
taking away a more meaningful learning gain this
week than last week?
NEIL   Yes. They didn't really learn anything the
previous week.
TUTOR   Aha. Do you think they know a bit more, and
that they were giving you back more by way of
feedback?
NEIL   Yes, definitely, I think they were more
interested than last week especially... when you can
make them laugh, sort of thing.
TUTOR   Aha, and you can't do that unless you are
using it naturally yourself. You know... you can't
laugh artificially - it's impossible to do really.
NEIL   Yes and I think you can make the pupils laugh
as well through your activities.
TUTOR   I think you know there is a lot of discovery
for you in that experience this week.
NEIL   Yes.
TUTOR   I think if you can catch hold of those two or
three fundamental things - and they are fundamentals
- and you know Vera found that out last week
actually for herself and you have found more or less
the same thing this week. The whole thing of
movement and expression and interest inside you as a
person only comes when the other things let it
happen. I think you have got something to build on
to now. Don't lose what you have gained there this
week. You can think about that for next week now
and we will be dealing with this next week. You now
know what you are after, don't you?

110

NEIL   Aha.
TUTOR   Lesson preparation, and how to teach concepts
... and how to structure a lesson from a logical
point of view, in order to create a context in which
you can behave as an ordinary person. But you still
have to work with the class.
NEIL   Hmm?
TUTOR   In terms of the way content's used as the
context in which all the other things happen, and
once you get that right, then you're - bang, you're
off! You didn't have much feedback from them
really, did you, in that lesson... in the closure to
your lesson?
NEIL   Well I think maybe I... had enough closure.
TUTOR   But I got the impression that you were doing
that for them. Did they really do much of it
themselves?
NEIL   I told them to write it down, to write it
down themselves.
TUTOR   Yes.
NEIL   And then when I walked round they couldn't
spell it so I knew then I was in trouble.
KEITH   I find that they can't spell... which means
that they can't really do a test.
JANET   You are better to give them questions and
everyone... get individual responses.
TUTOR   Ahah.
(All four students then moved into a fairly lengthy
analysis among themselves as to how to get the
pupils involved in the lesson. The tutor did not
interrupt but allowed the interaction to continue
until it appeared to come to a natural end.)
TUTOR   Well you broke it down there. I think you
managed that well today, but the lesson was set up
to be an exposition lesson. Well you know, for
example, you hadn't much questioning in the lesson.
NEIL   Yes it's true. I didn't ask very many
questions.
TUTOR   You had a lot of teacher telling.
NEIL   Yes.
TUTOR   Now you could quite usefully think to try and
get away from that a bit, and try to get more
variety in terms of the teaching strategies that you
want to include.
NEIL   Involve the pupils more?
TUTOR   Aha.
NEIL   Yes, I'll try to get the pupils doing
something.
TUTOR   Well that's it. Try to get away from this
straight exposition all the time.
NEIL   I thought that I might use worksheets.

TUTOR Yes, well you could do that, as long as you
had it well prepared, so that it was within their
ability.
NEIL   Yes, something simple.
TUTOR Well you have still time to think about that.
The important thing is not to lose hold of the gains
you have made.

Excerpt 4

Excerpt 4 was drawn from a lengthy review conference
(well in excess of 2 hours) supervised by a IIB
tutor. Lesson 4 was under review. The IIB nature
of the discussions was guided by the tutor's
questioning strategy which showed a valuing of
students' opinions and a redirecting of questions
around the group in order to develop understanding.
The students were being challenged to think about
teaching in terms of relationships with the
children. Very few tutor opinions were offered
directly, but the tutor's views were being
expressed, being implied in a subtle way through the
interactive style. The tutor did not offer any
specific suggestions for improvement. The student
identified a problem with a pupil, Colin, and this
was taken up by the tutor as a means of focusing the
students on the differences that exist between
pupils.

TUTOR Well, what did you make of Colin's reaction
to that? You can see the reaction was interesting
in that here was quite a contrast or reversal of
role between Colin and Nigel. What do you put that
down to?
PETER I don't think that he wanted to study. When
we went in he said, 'Can we draw today?' - that was
before I went in for my lesson.
TUTOR Yes. (Pause) And you told him, as it were?
PETER Yes, we probably did.
TUTOR So you think he was saving himself for that?
PETER He seemed to be waiting patiently.
TUTOR Whether or not he was interested in the
actual topic, he wasn't interested in playing a
part? He wasn't in that sense involved, in the way
that others were in answering you? He was quite
happy to sit back and allow everybody else to do the
answering for a change?
PETER Maybe he thought it was too simple for them.
He could see the point.
TUTOR Would you start to get anxious about that? -

You personally?
JOAN   Ahm-mm, I would.
TUTOR   What about you, Jane?
JANE   The problem of not answering?
TUTOR   Ahm-mm, how would you feel about him being
there? Would you feel that you would want to gallop
him into doing something? Or would you just shrug
your shoulders?
JANE   You would want him to take an interest in it
because it would... he would distract the rest of
the class.
TUTOR   He wasn't doing it there. He was just
sitting around.
PETER   Perhaps not in that case but he would do.
TUTOR   He was in other cases, yes. So you would
want to get him involved?
JANE   Yes.
TUTOR   How would you do it?
PETER   I think I would ask him stuff, so I would.
TUTOR   Direct questions? If he gave you a joke
response as he seems to be in favour of there...
what would you do then?
DAVID   I think you would clamp down on Colin...
because Kieran doesn't answer. I think maybe that
was... he kept telling us we should keep quiet and
everything while he sat with them and 'you could do
without me'.
TUTOR   I think that's quite possible, aha aha.
DAVID   Because it even happens... if you only
mention... He can't take it if anyone says, 'Sit
down and keep quiet'. He can't sit down and be able
to keep quiet... He'll go to the extreme.
TUTOR   Yes. Well, 'If you don't like my
contribution I am not going to make any'.
PETER   Yes. He won't want anyone to give it to you.
I think he would be temperamental alright.
TUTOR   How do you explain this transformation in
Nigel?
JOAN   Being at the front.
TUTOR   So Colin when he's moved to the front becomes
a problem, but not with Nigel when he was moved to
the front. It's very important that, isn't it? Is
that how you put them in the room?
JOAN   It wouldn't affect the girls really so much;
there's really not much difference in them.
TUTOR   Well, would you say so?
JOAN   I felt that the two at the back... and
they're that kind of... if they get a general chance
at all, they are talking to each other, laughing,
giggling.
TUTOR   I felt this on previous weeks that they do

this a bit.
PETER   Fiona will do this no matter where she is,
wherever she's around she'll talk.
TUTOR   But she tends to stay out of it?
JANE   I would say Kerry didn't as much either, as
Naomi was laughing you know. I read a wee story and
she was laughing at it the previous week and I took
her hands down twice and she was still... Whenever I
took it on she came in again.
TUTOR   Well, it's some kind of wee trick she's got.
JANE   Aha. Yes... (indistinguishable)... on each
side of her.
TUTOR   Aha. O.K. Let's take another look at the
videotape.

CONCLUSIONS

These descriptive studies have used a variety of
research methods to explore student-tutor
interpersonal relationships in microteaching review
conferences. The results would suggest that the
type of interpersonal relationships established is
related to the tutor's aims and approach and is an
influential factor, as Figure 6.1 illustrates, in
determining whether or not the students become
sensitised to the role of the affective domain in
teaching and learning. The students have available
as comparisons the affective meanings of their own
interpersonal relationships as teacher in the
microlessons and as learner in the review
conference. In the case of TCD tutors this
comparison was brought to the fore and the business
of learning to teach was very much a personal
exploration, whereas PCT tutors paid scant attention
to personal development. In particular, the
indirect/direct approaches of the two groups of
tutors illustrated this difference, which was
reflected in the students' perceptions of their
relationships with their tutors as revealed in the
student interviews and by the small differences in
the SRI scores. These differences in SRI scores
were not statistically significant, but the groups
did differ significantly in the extent to which they
considered their supervision, as measured by SCATS,
to be helpful.

Fig. 6.1: Students' affective learning opportunities

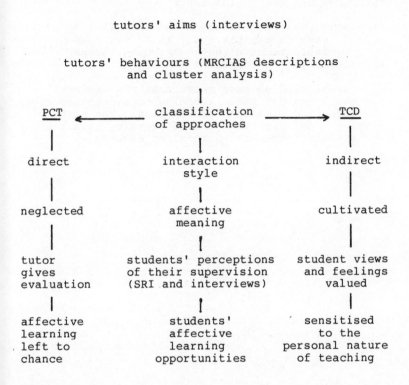

In all kinds of ways the students were sensing the attitudes and approach of their supervisor. They were continually making judgements about the tutor's motives and about their relationships with him. They were hesitant to reveal their own feelings when the tutor emphasised the evaluation of their teaching, especially when this evaluation consisted of negative criticism.

"He's providing enough ammunition of his own without me giving him more." (Student supervised by a IA tutor)

In these circumstances the students operated just by responding to the tutor's leads, a situation that IA and IB tutors misinterpreted:

"It's almost impossible to get students to evaluate their own lessons." (IA tutor)

"For some reason the students are not willing or able to make judgements about their own lessons. It's probably because they don't have enough experience yet." (IB tutor)

These studies have shown that the students certainly had different learning opportunities about the affective dimension of teaching. The next chapter considers the types of learning gain that the students were making in microteaching.

Chapter 7.

HOW STUDENTS LEARN IN MICROTEACHING

Two avenues of exploration had been followed in
investigating students' learning in microteaching.
If students were making progress in their
performance of teaching skills and were developing
their understanding of teaching and their skills in
self-evaluation, then this ought to be apparent from
their responses to the Student Post Teaching
Questionnaire (SPTQ). This open-ended questionnaire
had been administered to all students on two
occasions in the Year 1 study immediately after they
had taught their lessons and before they viewed the
videorecordings. SPTQ asked students for their
opinions about the lesson they had just taught. A
stratified sample of students had also been
interviewed on two occasions in the Year 1 study and
one of the purposes of these interviews had been to
find out how they felt they were learning in
microteaching. Figure 7.1 describes the various
stages of the investigation.
     Viewing and discussing the recorded microlesson
presents the learner to 'himself as teacher' and
provides one major influence on the type of learning
that the student experiences. The use of
videorecordings as feedback has generated
considerable interest and argument in research
circles, the discussion being generally focused on
the effects and outcomes of seeing and hearing
oneself teach - the act of 'self-confrontation'.
Researchers have disagreed as to the influence and
effects of self-confrontation, (e.g. Fuller and
Manning, 1973; Travers, 1975; Finlayson, 1975;
MacLeod, 1976b, 1977; Griffiths, 1974, 1977). The
association of self-confrontation with mechanical
feedback may be unnecessarily restrictive in
understanding its role in microteaching. We believe
that self-confrontation in microteaching may be

117

Fig. 7.1: Investigating how students were learning
in microteaching

Student teaches the lesson

Specific issues of lesson experience
    self-confrontation identified

Are any of these issues   What percentage of
taken up in the review ——YES—— the SPTQ issues
    conference?   are discussed?

    NO

Other issues discussed

    S T U D E N T   A T T I T U D E S
    (Student interviews - SPCI)

    which may be reflected in

    SCATS   SRI   SPTQ Quality Analysis

a two stage process, involving firstly the
experience of actually teaching the lesson, and
secondly that of viewing the videorecorded lesson in
the supervised review conference. Although the
influence of the lesson experience on
self-confrontation has never been seriously taken up
in any previous microteaching research, its presence
has been acknowledged:

> After the taping and before the playback, the
> person privately evaluates his performance and
> identifies discrepancies between his
> experienced performance and his goal. This is
> his satisfaction with his performance. The
> content of these discrepancies is likely to
> resemble the teacher's current concerns. The
> size of these discrepancies is likely to
> influence the positiveness and negativeness of
> his attitudes towards playback before it

occurs, and to influence both his motivation to change and the actual effects of the playback. (Fuller and Manning, 1973, p.510)

Many of the experienced microteaching tutors at the New University of Ulster, particularly those whose aims were classified as Teaching Concept Development, seemed well aware of the need to take account of the student's own experiences of having taught the lesson. As one supervisor put it:

"Some people assume that the videotape that is being reviewed is something new and different. In fact it's not. The student who taught the lesson has already experienced it and will be looking for certain things... So, a review for the individual is always a focused review, because she's taught the lesson. She knows what it felt like. Now, those are the things she wants to have a look at, because... it went well today... and, there's something else she wants to look at because she wasn't able to handle that. She'll want to think more about that too." (TCD, IIA tutor)

Something important has already happened before the student attends the review conference. The student has feelings and some understanding of the relative success of his lesson as a result of having taught it. Thus, without the aid of a videorecording, he is in a position to fault himself on certain aspects of his teaching and to experience satisfaction with other parts of the lesson that seemed to have worked particularly well. Are the issues discussed during the review conference the student's own concerns and satisfactions, or do they, in fact, originate from the tutor's experience of watching the videotaped lesson? If the former is true then the student's lesson-experience self-confrontation is being valued. TCD tutors had argued that they did take the student's experiences of the lesson into account. Is the use of lesson-experience self-confrontation to focus the review discussions a strategy which discriminates Teaching Concept Development tutors from the other supervisors? These questions formed the basis of the first enquiry: the investigation of lesson-experience self-confrontation as a means of focusing the review conference discussions.

TCD tutors, in their aims interviews, had indicated that they wanted a student-focused review in order to encourage students to analyse their own teaching experiences and to develop a personal understanding of teaching. Do students develop the ability to analyse their own teaching over the series of microteaching lessons and review conferences? Is this ability then reflected in the quality of the students' post teaching self-evaluations? Do students supervised by TCD tutors differ from the other students in this respect? These questions formed the basis of the second enquiry: the investigation of the quality of the students' lesson-experience self-confrontations.

LESSON-EXPERIENCE SELF-CONFRONTATION AND THE FOCUS OF REVIEW CONFERENCE DISCUSSIONS

This study concerned the extent to which the students' lesson experience self-confrontations were followed up in the review conference. Immediately after the teaching of Lesson 3/4 and Lesson 6/7, the Student Post Teaching Questionnaire (SPTQl and SPTQ2) was administered to the total population of students. The SPTQ was derived from the work of MacLeod (1976a) and of Millar and McIntyre (1977). It invited students to respond to the question, 'How do you feel about the lesson you have just taught?' by writing down "those reactions which pleased or dissatisfied you". Students were asked to take a new paragraph for each separate issue mentioned. All of the students' SPTQl and SPTQ2 responses were subsequently subjected to quality analysis.

The SPTQl and SPTQ2 responses of the 64 students in the review groups of the 16 tutors in the Year 1 study were retrieved, and the issues discussed therein were identified. Next, the 32 audio-recorded review conferences of these groups were listened to in order to establish if the students' self-declared issues were taken up in the review conference discussions. Table 7.1 shows the mean percentage uptake in the review conferences of the students' issues as declared in their SPTQ responses.

Students supervised by TCD tutors were much more likely to have their post teaching concerns and satisfactions discussed in the review conference than students supervised by PCT tutors. Also, as the microteaching programme progressed the TCD tutors gave their students greatly increased responsibility for identifying the topics for discussion. A similar comparison was made for the students supervised by Educational Studies and

Curriculum Methods tutors but there was little difference in the up-take of students' issues in these two groups of conferences.

Table 7.1: Percentage of students' issues discussed

Students grouped by tutors' aims	% of issues discussed	
	SPTQ1	SPTQ2
IA	30%	34%
IB	27%	50%
IIA	58%	90%
IIB	64%	92%

A sample of 32 students had been interviewed following each of the recorded review conferences (Student Post Conferences Interviews, SPCI1 and SPCI2). SPCI1 specifically sought to determine the students' reactions to the extent to which the issues identified by the students in SPTQ1 had been discussed in the review conferences. The interviews revealed that the students were very aware as to whether or not tutors made room for discussion of the student's own concerns. The vignettes of the interviews presented in Chapter Six have illustrated this awareness. Indeed, the provision of opportunities to follow up their lesson-experience self-confrontation was a major factor that the students considered in judging the effectiveness of their supervision.

THE QUALITY OF THE STUDENTS'
LESSON-EXPERIENCE SELF-CONFRONTATION

TCD tutors had argued that the issues discussed in the review conference ought to come from the students because this would aid their personal development as teachers, thereby enabling them to develop the range of concepts and the language to apply in evaluating their own teaching. If students were developing their self-evaluative abilities, then this ought to be reflected in the quality of their Student Post Teaching Questionnaire (SPTQ)

responses. Swallow (1984) has described the
development of a system for analysing the reponses
to the SPTQ in order to indicate the depth of each
student's perceptions and evaluations of his own
microlesson. Appendix D summarises the system.
Each statement made by the student was coded in four
dimensions in terms of Substantive Category,
Self-critique, Thinking in Explaining and
Self-appreciation, as outlined in Figure 7.2.

Fig. 7.2: The SPTQ Analysis System

1. Substantive Categories
The kinds of issue on which the student focused were
classed as:
 1.1 Learning experiences
  (a) The weekly teaching skill
  (b) Other teaching skills
  (c) The lesson
  (d) The pupils
 1.2 The microteaching system and organisation
 1.3 Me (affect and self-regard) only

2. Self-critique
The comments were coded in terms of:
 (a) Value weighting - i.e. use of self-analysis
  (none, positive, negative, or balanced)
 (b) Affect - i.e. personal feelings included
  (yes, no)
 (c) Progress - i.e. indicated improvement (yes,
  no)

3. Thinking in Explaining
Each statement was categorised as either:
 (a) Non-relational - i.e. contained simple
  descriptive reporting and unsubstantiated
  opinions, or
 (b) Relational - i.e. included reason-giving
  explanation

4. Self-application
Each statement was coded as belonging to one of
three categories:
 (a) A general statement
 (b) A lesson specific statement
 (c) A statement which linked the specific
  experience of the lesson to a
  generalisation.

The results from this analysis were interpreted in terms of the depth of thinking that students were applying to themselves as teachers. In particular, it was possible to distinguish lower level thinking (description and opinion) and higher level thinking (application, analysis and evaluation) in a manner similar to that of Bloom's Taxonomy of Educational Objectives - Cognitive Domain (1956). Bloom had discriminated between judgements that could be classified as 'true' evaluations and those which were simply opinions:

> for the most part, the evaluations customarily made by an individual are quick decisions not preceded by very careful consideration of the various aspects of the objects, idea, or activity being judged. These might more properly be termed opinions rather than judgements. (p.186)

Lower level thinking by students would yield SPTQ responses which were confined to descriptive observations and simple expressions of 'opinion'. In terms of the dimensions generated for the SPTQ Analysis System, such statements would not show any evidence of relational thinking (Thinking in Explaining dimension) and would be concerned with either consideration of the lesson just taught, or, some aspect of teaching in general (Self-application dimension). With regard to the dimension of Self-critique, descriptive reporting would be expected to be expressed in objective terms (i.e. without value weighting), and opinion, though value weighted, may be limited to the cognitive, impersonal consideration of issues.

The use of higher level thinking in SPTQ responses would involve the ability to generalise from the immediate teaching experience and to apply this generalisation in an appropriate context (Self-application dimension, specific-general linking). Evidence of analytical thinking would be indicated by the semantic complexity of the statements, with the students using such structures as a way of employing language to demonstrate their depth of understanding (Thinking in Explaining dimension, relational). Structurally complex statements, upon which no value weighting was placed would demonstrate analysis but not evaluation. Where there was Self-critique at the 'Cognitive only' level, this would signal the move from analysis to evaluation. With 'Cognitive only' critique the student would not be attempting to define himself into the situation, i.e. it would be an appraisal of the event, not of himself within the event. Self-critique at the level of 'Cognitive, with affect' would still be an intellectual consideration, but since it is expressed with affect, it would demonstrate a highly personal involvement. The statement would be expressed in terms of the student's own feelings, and when such expressions involve analysis the student would be supplying evidence of thinking that is deeply intellectual about "me and my experience". Semantically complex statements, containing 'Cognitive and Affect, with Progress' would indicate the highest level of understanding, demonstrating that the student was not seeing the lesson as an isolated experience, that microteaching was about the whole experience of what was happening to him, giving evidence of growing conceptualisation and personal model building.

Students who had tutors whose prime objective was that of encouraging the student teacher to analyse his experience of himself as a teacher in order to build a personal conceptualisation of teaching (i.e. the declared aims of the IIA and IIB tutors) would be expected to demonstrate a higher level of thinking skills than students whose tutors require less student self-analysis. It was thus anticipated that students, whose tutors had been classified as TCD, would demonstrate a greater proportion of higher level thinking skills in their SPTQ responses than students whose tutors have been classified as PCT.

The SPTQ results
The Substantive Categories
For all student groups the largest proportion of themes was concerned with learning experiences, as Table 7.2 shows.

Table 7.2: % of SPTQ themes on learning experiences

Student groups	SPTQ1	SPTQ2
IA tutored students	69%	81%
IB tutored students	83%	79%
IIA tutored students	91%	94%
IIB tutored students	71%	73%

12% of both PCT and TCD tutored students responded with more than 5 themes categorised as learning experiences in their SPTQ1 responses. However, the SPTQ2 returns revealed important differences. Only 4% of the students supervised by IA tutors, and only 2% of the students supervised by IB tutors responded with more than 5 themes about learning experiences, compared to 12% of the IIA tutored students and 21% of the IIB tutored students. Within the learning experiences sub-categories the students paid little attention to the weekly skill, the largest figure of 3% being recorded for the SPTQ1 responses of the IA tutored students. This finding was consistent with the MRCIAS systematic analysis results of the review conference discussions.

For those themes which were categorised as microteaching system and organisation, three aspects appeared to predominate. 5% of both the PCT and TCD tutored students' responses focused on the supervisor, illustrating the central position occupied by the tutor in terms of the students' experiences of microteaching. Concerns about the pupils were expressed by some students intent on teaching secondary school pupils, but who were obliged to teach primary school pupils in microteaching. This theme was mentioned in 4% of the themes listed by the PCT tutored students but in only 0.5% of the TCD tutored students' themes (a difference that was to be expected from the tutors' aims interviews and the MRCIAS analysis of the review conference discussions). Some students discussed the fact that microlessons were confined to 15 minutes (4% of the themes mentioned by the PCT tutored students and 3% of the TCD tutored students' themes). However the student interviews indicated that students quickly adapted to the short lesson, and this aspect of the programme was not an important issue. About 5% of the themes from both PCT and TCD tutored students were confined to expressions of 'Myself and how I feel'.

Self-critique Steady use was made of self-analysis (value weighting) in the students' responses. In both the SPTQ1 and SPTQ2 responses the students expressed a predominantly positive self-critique. Only minor differences were found in the value weighting of SPTQ1 and SPTQ2 for all student groups. The proportion of students' expressions of feelings about their experience, categorised as expressions of affect, were different for PCT and TCD tutored

students. The percentage of statements containing
expressions of affect remained fairly stable at
around 40% from occasion to occasion for those
students supervised by PCT tutors. Students
supervised by TCD tutors gave appreciably fewer
statements containing affect in SPTQ2 (25%) as
compared to SPTQ1 (45%), reflecting a move towards a
more objective approach in their writing - an
unexpected finding.

As regards expressions of progress, except for
the SPTQ1 responses of students supervised by IA
tutors, where a relatively high figure of 43% was
recorded, stable patterns of around 30% of themes
containing 'progress' were found to exist in the
SPTQ1 and SPTQ2 responses for both the students
supervised by PCT and TCD tutors. The 43% figure
for the IA tutored students was surprising
considering the findings from the student interviews
which indicated a general dissatisfaction of the
strategy adopted by the IA tutors in conference. If
such students have judged the review conference as
unhelpful it would seem probable that the majority
of learning gains would result from the teaching
experience rather than from the review conference.
If such a situation did in fact exist then the
concept of progress would be of primary importance.

Thinking in Explaining The contrasting trends in
the data with regard to the Thinking in Explaining
dimension were very interesting. Students
supervised by PCT tutors produced a greater
proportion of themes classified as relational
thinking in their SPTQ2 responses (57%) than in
their SPTQ1 responses (46%). Thus it would appear
that students supervised by PCT tutors have shown
increased use of self-evaluation after the 3-week
period.

However, for the students supervised by TCD
tutors the trends were reversed. While the SPTQ1
responses provided evidence of more higher level
thinking (67%) than even the SPTQ2's of the PCT
tutored students, the results indicated a sharp
decline in use of higher level thinking in the SPTQ2
responses (37%). How could this be explained? Why
have the students supervised by TCD tutors not
maintained the high proportion of relational themes?
The MRCIAS analysis had revealed that students
supervised by TCD tutors were involved in a
predominantly indirect approach where students were
continually being encouraged to analyse the nature
of teaching and their experiences of themselves as

teachers. Also, these students expressed very positive attitudes to the strategy adopted by their supervisors and were very aware of their own learning and progress in understanding teaching. After 6 or 7 weeks of this kind of supervision it would appear possible that the students had shifted their thinking beyond the immediate lesson to the complexities of teaching and to examining their own personal values as career teachers.

Self-application   Table 7.3 shows the percentage distribution of themes across the three Self-application categories of general statements (1), lesson specific statements (2) and specific to general linked statements (3).

Table 7.3: Distribution of self-application themes

Student groups	Occasion	Categories		
		1	2	3
IA tutored students	SPTQ1	23%	56%	21%
	SPTQ2	10%	76%	14%
IB tutored students	SPTQ1	21%	47%	32%
	SPTQ2	17%	70%	13%
IIA tutored students	SPTQ1	6%	55%	39%
	SPTQ2	6%	86%	8%
IIB tutored students	SPTQ1	14%	48%	38%
	SPTQ2	25%	59%	16%

Students supervised by both PCT and TCD tutors responded with more general-lesson specific linked statements (Category 3, hypothesised as evidence of higher level thinking) in their SPTQ1's than in their SPTQ2's. Higher figures were obtained for TCD tutored students than PCT tutored students. In terms of the number of themes per student for each category, one notable characteristic emerged. Only those students supervised by TCD tutors produced more than three general-lesson specific linked statements in their SPTQ1 responses (14% of the IIA tutored students, and 12% of the IIB tutored students).

STUDENTS' PERCEPTIONS OF MICROTEACHING

In the second set of interviews (SPCI2) the sample
of students was asked about the learning gains that
they felt they were making in microteaching and
about the aspects of microteaching to which these
learning gains could be attributed. Also, students
were asked about their future development in terms
of their aims and needs, the objective being to see
if their aims were in keeping with their tutors'
views of the purposes of microteaching as being
either for immediate practical gains or for long
term affective and cognitive gains. The students'
responses are summarised in terms of their tutors'
aims as being either Practice for Classroom Teaching
(PCT) or Teaching Concept Development (TCD)

Students supervised by PCT tutors

The microteaching experiences of students supervised
by IA tutors were very similar to those of students
supervised by IB tutors. This was not surprising in
view of the results obtained from the MRCIAS and
cluster analyses of the verbal behaviours of the
review conference groups. These students felt that
microteaching had allowed them to develop
self-confidence through improving their lesson
planning and teaching skills by working with real
learners. The students appreciated the opportunity
to experiment in the use of a wide range of teaching
strategies and aids. The videotape was regarded as
a necessary and useful feedback device for studying
their own teaching and comparing it with that of
their peers.

The students reported that the skill of the
week had been largely ignored in the review
conference discussions. This was particularly
interesting with regard to the IA tutors who claimed
in their initial interviews to take the weekly skill
exercises into account as a means of linking the
lecture programme with the review conference. IA
tutors were reported to encourage their students to
integrate the microteaching exercises from the
lectures into their lesson plans, whereas IB tutors
did not take the weekly skill into account in the
discussions. The IA tutored students seemed both
surprised and relieved that the microteaching
exercises were not emphasised in the review
conferences, while the IB tutored students were
happy to ignore them from the outset. However, all
16 students supervised by the PCT tutors viewed the
lectures as purposeful in helping them with criteria

for planning and in indicating those aspects of their teaching which were worthy of attention.

PCT tutors, in their initial interviews, had stressed the inexperience of the students. They had described their role as that of the experienced staff member who discriminated the specific strengths and weaknesses of their students' teaching, particularly in view of the fact that their next teaching encounter would be the major block practice in the schools. Without exception, the students did not find this a valuable way to proceed. They claimed to know themselves what problems they were having, and described the approach that their tutors favoured as being rigid and uncompromising. More seriously perhaps, this promoted a feeling that the tutor was distant and unapproachable. Students wanted to talk about their concerns but felt that the atmosphere did not allow it. Some students found this very upsetting while others grew to accept the tutor's strategy as normal procedure and that the means of their success in microteaching (i.e. achieving a good grade) lay in the extent to which they could produce a performance consistent with the tutor's ideas of what was a good lesson. Thus it would appear that a mismatch existed between the tutors' understanding of the needs of the inexperienced students and the genuine desires and expectations of the students with regard to the purpose and potential of the review conference.

Students supervised by TCD tutors

All 16 students supervised by TCD tutors emphasised the influence that the review conferences exerted on what they had learned from the experience of microteaching. They regarded their tutors highly for their flexibility and sensitivity toward them as individuals. The experiences of teaching the lessons and viewing the recordings were both regarded as valuable for providing the issues for discussion. The students did not consider the tutors' persistent quests for analysis to be threatening; rather, they appreciated that this was a valuable means of probing the complexities of teaching. Students praised their supervisors' ability to employ the group dynamics of the situation in a way that united them as a team with common aspirations. However, despite the TCD tutors' consensus aims, differences in emphasis were apparent in the IIA and IIB tutored students' views.

Students supervised by IIA tutors described

their gains in terms of lesson planning, organisational skills, and in providing successful learning experiences for the pupils. What was surprising was that this was reminiscent of the focus brought to the review conferences by the PCT (IA and IB) tutors. Could it be that the PCT and IIA tutors had similar understandings of classroom teaching despite their dissimilarity in supervisory approach?

In contrast, students supervised by IIB tutors identified a very different exphasis in the thrust provided by the tutor:

"... obviously learning is what it is all about but for us as microteaching students it doesn't come over as the reason for the review conference. It's a big relationship thing. It's how they are reacting to you and how you are reacting to them..."

Could it be that the IIB tutors view the nature of classroom teaching differently from the other tutors?

CONCLUSIONS

The extent to which students' lesson experience self-confrontations were employed to focus the review conferences was investigated. Students supervised by TCD tutors were more likely to have their post teaching concerns and satisfactions discussed in the review conferences than students supervised by PCT tutors. Students supervised by PCT tutors described their review conferences as almost entirely controlled by the tutors, in contrast to the TCD tutored students who experienced their review conferences as open to student direction. Also, the TCD tutored students appeared to have more regard for their supervisors than the PCT tutored students, with the student interviews (SPCI1) revealing a relationship between the students' affective perceptions of their supervisor and the approach that the tutor adopted.

We have also reported a brief summary of the results from the analysis of the range and quality of the students' responses to the Student Post Teaching Questionnaires (SPTQ1 and SPTQ2). Little attention was given to the weekly skill, with the largest proportion of issues being concerned with learning experiences (i.e. teaching behaviours, the pupils, and the lesson). Both SPTQ1 and SPTQ2 responses showed a predominance of positive critique, indicating that the students found their microteaching experiences reassuring and felt they were progressing.

With regard to the quality of responses, students supervised by PCT tutors displayed increased use of self-evaluation after the 3-week period. However, while the SPTQ1 responses of the TCD tutored students provided evidence of more higher level thinking than even the SPTQ2 responses of the PCT tutored students, a sharp decline was observed in their SPTQ2 responses. It was hypothesised that these results were related to the TCD tutors' long term aims for microteaching and that these students were focusing on the complexities of teaching and on themselves as career teachers, rather than on the lesson just taught.

The students' experiences of microteaching were greatly influenced by the practice of their individual tutors. Students supervised by PCT tutors derived most of their gains from the teaching experiences (confidence in planning and presentation, experience with classroom aids etc.), and from the opportunity that the videotape allowed for viewing their own teaching and comparing it with that of their peers. The supervisor was described as an evaluator and assessor who sought to eliminate poor teaching and reinforce that which he regarded as good teaching.

In contrast, students supervised by TCD tutors identified the review conference as the major source of learning. They liked and respected their tutors for the value they appeared to place on them as individuals, and experienced microteaching as a means of developing personal foundations for a future career in teaching. The supervisor continually asked the students for their opinions, he compared and contrasted the differing approaches, he integrated these with his own experiences of theory and practice, but most of all, he avoided absolute judgements.

What were the origins of these distinctly differing approaches to the supervision of microteaching? Could it be that the PCT tutors enter microteaching with a different understanding of their role in preparing student teachers for their future careers than did the TCD tutors?

There was close agreement in the perceptions of students supervised by the PCT tutors and those supervised by the TCD, IIA tutors with regard to what they were learning about teaching. Teaching was described as a skilled activity, its purpose being to provide organised learning experiences for the pupils from which they would derive definite gains. In contrast, students supervised by IIB tutors displayed different perceptions of teaching. They discussed the children in the class, interpreted the motives of individual pupils, and generally appeared to account for teaching as a personal human activity relating with children.

Is it possible that the IIB supervisors enter microteaching with a different perspective or understanding of teaching to that of the other supervisors? The research may be exposing points of similarity and contrast in the supervisors' personal constructs for teaching and for the preparation of teachers.

Chapter 8.

MODELS OF MICROTEACHING

The research studies outlined so far have shown that
microteaching supervisors were adopting stable
approaches which were consistent with their aims,
and that these approaches were very influential in
determining the nature of students' learning in
microteaching. The interviews with tutors and
students had established that the tutors' aims and
approaches actually represented different
definitions of microteaching and had raised the
possibility that these definitions might be derived
from different personal construct systems for
teaching and teacher preparation. The Year 1
studies had indicated that tutors explained their
approach to their students in the first few review
conferences and so it was decided to follow the work
of a sample of tutors closely in the first few weeks
of microteaching (see Study 3, Year 2 in Chapter
Four for an outline of the research design).
      The first four review conferences of the sample
of eight tutors were audiotaped and examined for
evidence of the ways in which the tutors presented
their understanding of microteaching to their
students. The tutors were then interviewed and
asked to explain their observed behaviours and their
approach to microteaching in terms of their views
about the nature of teaching and teacher
preparation. Their groups of students were also
interviewed and asked about those specific
characteristics of their tutors' aims and practice
that had been identified from the audiorecordings
and the tutor interviews. The students were asked
about any student-tutor contacts outside of the
review conferences. These three sources were used
as a form of triangulation to provide supportive
evidence for eliciting the different definitions of
microteaching being implemented. In order to

interpret the tutors' views and practices revealed by this research the following contemporary models of teaching and teacher preparation were applied as conceptual frameworks.

MODELS OF TEACHING AND TEACHER PREPARATION

Models of teaching
The recent thrusts for accountability in all aspects and levels of education have fuelled the behaviourism-humanism debate about teaching.

> Each year we permit a teacher to function without gauging the consequences of that teacher's efforts on youngsters, we run the risk that another group of pupils has been swindled. This kind of unaccountable teaching must cease. (Popham, 1977, p.61)

Behaviourists have described efficient teaching in terms of its organisational clarity, which requires a rational approach to planning and assessment. Competent teachers, they have said, plan their lessons carefully, always bearing in mind precisely what it is that their pupils are expected to gain from the experience.

> Educators who are willing to subject their instructional efforts to scrutiny based on the subsequent behaviors of pupils could be said to endorse a form of behaviorism... (We) urge educators to formulate their objectives in terms of measurable pupil behaviors rather than the traditionally vague goal-statements previously employed. (Popham, 1977, p.60)

Since all of the teacher's decisions are based on his observations of the pupils' behaviours, the teacher (and others) should be in a position to assess formally the gains that the pupils have made. Thus behaviourists are concerned with the clear definition of teaching objectives, cognitive, affective and psychomotor, and with the assessment of the extent to which these objectives have been achieved. The onus is placed on educational research to improve the range and sophistication of the assessment procedures.

The objectives communicate the teacher's intentions and reduce a complex whole to a set of more manageable components. Teaching methods are

134

often referred to as methods of instruction, a subtle implication that a transmission mode of teaching is favoured. Other important characteristics of this model of teaching are that the means (i.e. the teaching activities) are separated from the ends (i.e. the teaching objectives), and that in planning the lesson, the ends precede the means.

Humanists have criticised the behaviourist performance-based model of teaching for its blind acceptance of the status quo (Nash and Agne, 1971) and for reducing education to the attainment of the most easily specifiable and observable objectives (Nash, 1970). Some critics have felt that the affective domain is neglected, with the vast majority of objectives being devoted to cognitive recall, and that, at its worst, this model of teaching produces individuals that are incapable of making independent decisions or of learning to think creatively (Pai and Krueger, 1979). It has also been pointed out that some very worthy goals are not measurable with present day techniques (Doll, 1979). In any case, specifying objectives does not, in itself, make a lesson argued Shepardson (1972).

Humanists do not suggest that knowledge and skills are unimportant but rather that these alone are not enough.

> Behavior... is only symptom, the causes of behavior lie in perceptions and beliefs... Behavior is a product of meaning... When a teacher perceives a child differently he behaves differently toward him... If we can be sure the teacher's ways of perceiving are accurate and constructive it may be necessary to know precisely how he will put his concern into effect. (Combs, 1972, pp.287,288)

The humanist model seeks to foster the processes by which pupils discover effective personal solutions to learning problems. The humanists' goals are concerned with aspects of education such as self-fulfilment, self-understanding, commitment, responsibility, adaptability and creativity. Doll (1979) has pointed out:

> ... that not all ends emerge before means (or conditions) are set, that not all ends, goals, purposes can be pre-determined, and that some ends can be articulated and measured only after

the experience or process has been lived
through. (p.337)

Thus, while the behaviourist enters the
teaching encounter with specific learning objectives
in mind, the humanist is not carrying any highly
specified objectives but is determined to respond to
the uniqueness of the situation and the pupils. The
behaviourist uses feedback to direct the learners
towards his objectives. The humanist employs
feedback to construct meaning as the basis for
action, what to teach and how to teach it. He is
continually concerned with what the pupils are
thinking and feeling, as well as doing. He observes
how they react to him and to each other. He is
sensitive to their life experience and its
relationship to the classroom environment and the
learning materials. Finally, the humanist teacher
appears to be always aware of his own reactions to
the pupils. The behaviourist seeks an organised
clarity before he begins to teach. The lessons are
pre-planned with specific objectives in mind, and
the total course of study may be described in terms
of the sum of its objectives. The humanist enters
the teaching situation as an observer, in which an
awareness of the children and himself grows and
develops. The resulting learning experience or
course of study is highly related and relevant to
the particular pupils concerned and is provided
within an intensely personalised teaching approach.
Concerns for both the teacher and the pupils
are expressed differently by behaviourists and
humanists. Behaviourists are concerned that the
teacher demonstrates mastery of a range of teaching
behaviours and skills, and that the pupils are
subjected to meaningful and definable learning
experiences. Humanists state that the acquisition
of knowledge and skills by the teacher is
insufficient. Rather, they tend to draw attention
to the teacher's values and beliefs, emphasising an
understanding of children and their motives. Combs
(1969) has argued that this focus on the personal
meaning for the teacher in wanting to teach results
in enormous gains for both the pupils and the
teacher.
Humanists have argued that the behaviourist
approach has not been found to be profitable:

Years of educational research ... indicates
that no single skill or group of skills, no
single competence or group of competencies, no

single trait or group of traits, no single
method or possession of mere knowledge alone
can be said to lead unerringly to effective
teaching. (Medeiros, Welch and Tate, 1979,
p.436)

Behaviourists accuse humanists of indulging in
rhetoric, and in the vague discussion of objectives
so wide-ranging that they become mere platitudes
(Watts, 1978). Some critics view humanists as
incapable of examining their own instructional
approaches, or unwilling to allow others to do so,
being content to assess their instructional
effectiveness according to whether they feel good
about it.

Humanism can offer a truly riskless position
for the teacher who does not wish to be
appraised. (Popham, 1977, p.60)

Cohen and Hersh (1972) have proposed a
syntheses of the behaviouristic and humanistic
models of teaching:

Rather than perpetuate the needless dichotomies
that characterize the discourse emanating from
both rigid behaviorism and naive humanism, we
propose a synthesis. (p.172)

They describe teaching as an intentional
activity, and state that what is required is an
increased sensitivity to the affective dimension of
teaching. They propose that behaviourists and
humanists together should construct a range of
objectives, and a rationale to support them, that
would allow evidence to be collected concerning the
extent to which the goals had been achieved.
Thoresen (1973) has suggested that a new field of
'behavioural humanism' is emerging. To humanists,
however, this is still essentially a behaviourist
model of teaching that takes insufficient account of
the humanistic approach.

Behaviorism and humanism are two theoretical
approaches for dealing with human events ...
Behaviorism and humanism cannot be synthesised.
The goal we seek is not to erase or ignore the
differences. On the contrary their special
values lie precisely in the fact of their
difference. What is needed is not synthesis,
but synchronization ... we need both frames of

reference. What is needed is persons who
understand both viewpoints sufficiently well to
know when and how to use them. (Combs, 1977,
pp.53,56)

Models of teacher preparation

Three different aspects of teacher preparation had
to be taken into account as conceptual frameworks to
apply to tutors' views and practices in
microteaching. First of all, student teachers are
learners and so contemporary learning theories can
be applied. Then, there are the various approaches
that have been advocated for teacher preparation,
and there is also the debate about whether teacher
preparation should involve education or training
processes.

Bigge (1982) has suggested that there are two
major families of contemporary learning theories,
the conditioning theories of the behaviourist family
and the cognitive theories of the Gestalt-field
family. He considered that the main distinction
between the two was that the behaviourist viewed the
learner as passive or reactive while the Gestaltist
viewed him as one who interacted with his
surrounding environment.

> In dealing with the following questions, a
> person orientated towards behaviourism is
> likely to give a significantly different answer
> from that given by a Gestalt-field theorist:
> What is intelligence? What happens when we
> remember and when we forget? What is
> perception? What is motivation? What is
> thinking? What is the role of practice in
> learning? How does learning transfer to other
> situations? (Bigge, 1982, p.49)

Behaviourists would claim that anyone can learn
anything of which he is capable provided that he
undertakes the programme of activities required for
conditioning to take place. It is assumed that
engaging the learner in certain behaviours in
conjunction with appropriate conditioning
automatically produces learning. In contrast,
Gestaltists speak of "psychological involvement" and
"the individual's need to learn". Attention is paid
to the earner's personal goals, it being considered
that learning without personal involvement produces
little more than a superficial, functional or
transitory learning gain.

138

A framework for considering approaches to the preparation of teachers has been provided by Terhart and Drerup (1981) who have identified three types of approach. The Craft Model stresses classroom experience and practice, and may be organised in the manner of an apprenticeship. Learning is achieved chiefly by imitating the well-tried strategies adopted by an experienced teacher. The Theory-to-Technology Model draws on the principles of behavioural psychology and scientific management techniques to focus on teacher performance, specified competencies and levels of accountability. The Enlightenment Model stresses an analytical approach to teacher preparation in which educational research and theory are used to aid the understanding, and thus the practice, of all those involved.

The different views about the roles of education and training in the processes of teacher preparation are illustrated by the following quotes.

> In teacher education, 'training' refers to that component of preparation for which departments and schools of education are specifically responsible. Such training is thus professionally or technically orientated in the sense that the skills and knowledge taught are supposed to have a direct bearing on professional practice. (Turner, 1975, p.97)

> Though training is an important ingredient in professional education, it is only an ingredient and not by any means the whole of it, or even the most important part of it in the long term. Being trained involves 'knowing how', being educated involves 'knowing that' as well as 'knowing how'. (Hilliard, 1971, pp.36,37)

Turner considered a teacher's education to consist of two separate components, that of his personal education (such as his degree specialism) and that of his preparation as a career teacher (teacher training). Hilliard focused on the teacher's professional studies and identified education and training as two useful concepts both of which were needed in the preparation of teachers. Wilson (1975) has argued that to be trained infers that the learning involves specific tasks and particular behaviours. Learning is achieved by practice, where the subject performs the task a little differently each time and observes or experiences the consequences. For the participant, theory is only minimally involved. On the other hand, Wilson has argued, to be 'educated' implies that the skill element and its practice, although important, are placed within a wider perspective which includes the consideration of relevant theories and principles.

> Not just anything counts as 'training' nor as 'education'... If the operation or type of learning involves... some sophisticated kinds of understanding, conceptual awareness or emotional response, 'train' becomes inappropriate - we do not train people to appreciate... or to love... or to become wise (even though certain types of training might be relevant to these ends). (Wilson, 1975, pp.107,108)

Relating the concepts of education and training to the two major families of contemporary learning theories and to the classification of approaches to teacher preparation yields two views about learning to teach.

(a) The training orientated view

While the Craft Model and Theory-to-Technology Model involve different approaches to teacher preparation they are both essentially behaviouristic and 'training' orientated. Practice provides experience, and experience is often matched with success. By serving a period as a classroom apprentice the advantage is that the new teacher will begin his career having acquired a minimum of coping strategies. The alternative way of providing this experience is through training in specified skills. However, the question remains as to whether the qualities required of a teacher can be learned through imitation or training. The main disadvantage of the 'training' concept is that it offers a predominantly fixed perspective of teaching and teaching methods, for without the resources of research and theory construction, changes only occur very slowly. Wilson (1975) has posed this question:

> What does the 'practice' or 'experience' part of teacher preparation give to teachers that they could not acquire for themselves anyway just by teaching? (p.134)

(b) The education orientated view

Terhart and Drerup's Enlightenment Model of teacher preparation is essentially cognitive in character in that it emphasises that changes in behaviour largely depend on the extent to which the teacher is 'enlightened' by his knowledge of educational theory, together with his analysis of himself as a teacher. Thus the point about the education concept is that it does not refute the benefits of practice and experience, but emphasises that lasting professional growth depends on knowledge, teacher self-analysis, and theory construction.

It is the process of theory construction which shapes the teacher's values and beliefs and hence his aims and perceptions, so that he comes to know himself as a teacher. This in turn makes him more aware of his own feelings towards his pupils and of the need to be sensitive to his pupils' feelings. An education orientated view of learning to teach is thus likely to include a humanistic perspective.

These, then, were the conceptual frameworks which were applied to interpret the tutors' models of microteaching and the origins of these models.

THE ORIGINS OF TUTORS' MODELS OF MICROTEACHING

The systematic observation of the early review conferences and the follow-up interviews of the tutors and their students reinforced the earlier findings that two different models of microteaching were in operation, namely Practice for Classroom Teaching (PCT) and Teaching Concept Development (TCD). In eliciting the relationships of these models to the tutors' views about teaching and teacher preparation it was found that the TCD IIA tutors and the TCD IIB tutors derived their approach from different sources. Thus the origins of PCT, TCD IIA and TCD IIB tutors' approaches need to be considered separately.

PCT tutors

The sample of four PCT tutors selected from the population of fifteen supervisors brought to microteaching a highly differentiated behaviouristic model of teaching that was distinctly evident not only in their expectations of their students' teaching behaviours, but also in their own teaching as microteaching supervisors. Several related aspects dominated their understanding of teaching.

The learning gains for the pupils had to be clearly defined. The favoured method of instruction was embedded in the need for domination and control. Assessment had two functions in teaching - that of establishing the extent to which the lesson objectives had been achieved, but also, more covertly, as a means of discipline and control.

"... There are two main points that I make at the beginning of microteaching. One is that whatever benefit they might get out of it, they should ensure that the children should actually learn something, that they should leave after that lesson having acquired some skill or knowledge which they didn't have before. The second thing I suggest to them is the importance of classroom management, even with small numbers of children... the importance of establishing that control from the outset."

The model of teacher preparation applied to microteaching by these tutors was one firmly rooted within a training orientation. They focused almost exclusively on teacher performance, viewing their role in terms of an expert-trainee relationship, in which the student was expected to demonstrate his developing behavioural expertise to his tutor.

"... For example, one of my students was talking about... I suppose it could be described as moral behaviour... questions about how they would react to certain situations. Now presumably the object of that lesson was to try and sensitise the children to the care and attention of other children. But of course there wasn't any actual direct teaching involved, and yet I had to mark that as an exercise."

"... The student has got to, or attempt to, direct his activities to please the supervisor, if only simply because he knows the supervisor in the end is going to assess him."

"... My initial remarks have also got another role and that is to let the students know what I expect from them, so that when it does come to assessment there will be no doubts as to what they are being assessed on."

TCD IIA tutors
Like the PCT tutors, the sample of two TCD IIA

tutors (from the population of four supervisors) brought to microteaching a model of teaching as a teacher dominated instructional activity, whose purpose and responsibility was that of providing appropriate learning experiences for pupils. The tutors exemplified this model in their own work. Their organisation and planning provided a well structured and conscientious teaching approach to microteaching supervision with the tutors accepting some responsibility for their students' learning gains.

"... The first stage in the early weeks is simply to get down to the business of lesson planning and to help them to see what constitutes a lesson. There has to be a structure to it... and there has got to be a coherence to it... and there has got to be an intellectual challenge for the children. It's not just fun and games, there's progress in here... and there's an expectation of learning to be taken out of each lesson. Sometimes I have had to work very hard to get a student to that stage. He now understands what lesson planning is all about. He now understands what makes a lesson, what constitutes a lesson, and he can build on that."

However, pupil control was not regarded in isolation from, or as a prerequisite for, instruction. Rather, good behaviour was regarded as the product of pupil interest, which had its basis in well-planned and stimulating learning activities.

"... I think there is a strong element of good organisation and good lesson planning required in order to let the relationships that you want develop in a situation in which they are going to be profitable. So there is naturally an intellectual challenge being put to the children all the time, as well as doing it in an atmosphere which allows mutual respect and trust. I don't think you can build one without the other."

The model of teacher preparation being applied to microteaching sharply contrasted with that of the PCT tutors. While the latter emphasised a predominantly behaviouristic approach, the TCD IIA tutors' model of teacher preparation was found to stress the importance of theoretical studies and teacher self-analysis for the discussion of teaching behaviour and for the construction of a personal

143

understanding of teaching. The review conference was regarded as the major source of learning rather than the limited practical experience component of the microlesson.

"... I don't think experience is worth having unless you are in a position to make good judgements of it. More of the same need not necessarily be a good thing. It is much more important to be able to help students evaluate themselves and their teaching than to give them plenty of practice at teaching. More doesn't necessarily mean better. More doesn't necessarily mean improvement. More can simply mean boredom. I don't think that we really intend to send them out as perfect teachers. I think we intend to send them out to the schools intending to continue learning to improve."

Thus the TCD IIA tutors emphasised the perception and analysis of teaching and they considered that microteaching offered an excellent opportunity to learn about teaching. This was an education or cognitive model of teacher preparation as opposed to the PCT tutors' model of practice and experience.

"... Also, I don't think you are in a position to evaluate your microteaching supervision unless you are carrying a fair set of assumptions about what teaching is, and about what learning is, and about what education is. You really carry those assumptions with you into your practice of microteaching. The way I behave will be coloured by what I think is important, which is determined by my depth of understanding of the many interrelated concepts involved."

TCD IIB tutors

The model of teaching that the sample of two tutors (from a population of eight TCD IIB supervisors) brought to microteaching was startlingly different from the others, who had described the activity of teaching in terms of the competent provision of effective learning experiences for the pupils. In contrast, the IIB tutors emphasised a shared teaching-learning environment, requiring teacher awareness and sensitivity. One interesting aspect of the IIB tutors was their knowledge and depth of understanding of what might be called the traditional or instructional model of teaching. It would seem possible that these tutors have moved beyond the limitations of such a model, to set up what one tutor called "contradictions" to a model of teaching that was "potentially exploitative... distorting... manipulative... coercive... destructive... and boring."

"... Teaching is about yourself. When I teach, what I am doing is that I am creating situations in which I'm learning. They are for my satisfaction, my creation, and because of my view of the way that human beings relate to one another, there always has to be somebody there to teach. Teaching is a language which implies dialogue, always with someone else, but it's about me, and the 'me' only exists in relation to somebody else. Therefore it's a paradigm case for me of what it means to be a human being. I am substantiated. I am made real. I am validated. It's a language, a metaphor for the notion of communication."

"... I want to reject the idea of providing learning experiences for anybody. I think that's just a more sophisticated version of control. What I am interested in is learning for myself; and when I talk to somebody else in such a way that I'm learning, then all sorts of things can happen for that person if they want them to happen, if they can engage with them. I'm providing a learning experience for myself - and I'm teaching."

"... I think teaching is an activity in which one is always in tension between the need to construct human relationships which are open, friendly, warm, happy - the claim is that that is the context in which people are open to learning - and the necessity that there has to be form, that the activity has to be a patterned activity, that there has to be sequences. There has to be some response to the imperatives in the situation - like time imperatives, like you can only hear one person talking at a time. What bothers me about the instructional model of teaching is that it maintains the social distances effectively. What I'm looking for is an acknowledgement of the tension between the two views, of a kind which generates what I want to call 'conversation' where the teacher doesn't deny his responsibility, and doesn't deny his authoritativeness. Walking that line seems to me to be a demanding human activity in its own right - but it's a common human activity. It's the problem we have in any relationship that is non-dominative. By being treated in that way children learn to become thinkers, enquirers, skilled human beings if you like, in terms of developing a kind of rational competence by discovering what it is to act rationally."

While the TCD IIB supervisors' model of teaching differed radically with that of the TCD IIA tutors, their models of teacher preparation applied to microteaching were similar. Both groups of tutors rejected a training orientated model of teacher preparation for microteaching, bringing instead an exploratory-analytical or education orientated model.

"... Microteaching brings together the two bits which many people struggle with: the pupil bit and the teacher bit. At one level they are the pupils with me as teacher. Then they go into the room and they switch to the teacher bit, and they handle this constant dichotomy back and forth. The change in them, in two dimensions, is condensed into this activity in the review room. It's a very powerful experience, the constant oscillations between power and powerlessness, between apparent strength and apparent weakness. What you have to do is to get both the strong and the weak bit together."

"... You must be willing to experience in some way the other person's anxiety, stress and uncertainty. I think that what you have to do all the time is that you have to push past fear, past a form of anxiety which has got distorted into fear to say, 'What went on? Something very strange happened there.' If they grapple with that question, and start constructing meaning out of it for themselves, then learning is taking place."

"... I knock on doors. My business is not to open the door and say, 'You must look at this!' I could do that. Sometimes you have to go knocking on a lot of doors before a door opens, which everybody goes through. I'm in the business of asking questions, all the time."

"... Somehow my objective is to get them to ask questions about everything that's going on in there. In order to really formulate some intellectual answer to the question, 'Why did I do what I did?' analysis is required on all kinds of levels. When you get to that stage you can ask a lot of questions, especially questions about what it is like in there teaching. I think that that's the central question that I want to keep in mind."

"... I'm attempting to construct with them a different language about what goes on in the room which is not pinned down or held in place by a language of achievement, the purpose of which is to help them develop personal criteria by which they can make sense of their teaching."

CONCLUSIONS

Figure 8.1 summarises the conclusions obtained from this research study. Both PCT and TCD, IIA tutors brought to microteaching a model of teacher as a competent instructor. They promoted an analysis of students' teaching in terms of the teacher's behavioural efficiency in providing worthwhile learning experiences for pupils. In contrast, TCD, IIB tutors brought to microteaching a humanistic model of teacher and they promoted the analysis of students' teaching in terms of a developing understanding of children and of the teacher in the role of building relationships with children.

PCT tutors used microteaching as a scaled down practice situation in which their supervision was based on teacher preparation as training and on the tutor's role in giving evaluative feedback. TCD tutors used microteaching as a teaching laboratory in which their supervision was based on teacher preparation as education, seeking long term gains in terms of cognitive understanding in the case of IIA tutors and affective sensitivity in the case of IIB tutors.

Fig. 8.1: The origins of tutors' personal construct systems for microteaching

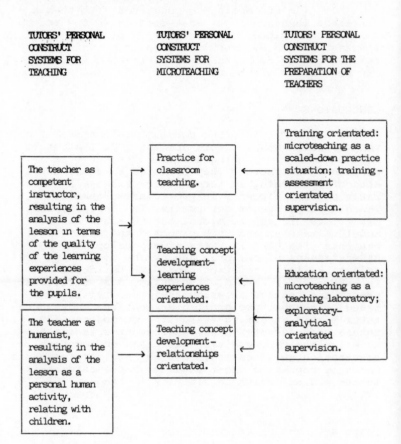

Chapter 9

MICROTEACHING: CONSTRUCTS, PROCESSES AND RATIONALE

RECENT DEVELOPMENTS IN MICROTEACHING RATIONALE

During the period in which this research was being
conducted microteaching continued to spread and the
rate of publication of articles on microteaching
appears to have been maintained. Malley and Clift
(1980) have provided a very useful review and
annotated bibliography, citing 772 selected
references up to 1978. Mohanty (1984) has listed
228 articles, mostly published between 1975 and
August 1983. A computer search of the Educational
Resources Information Centre (ERIC) system for the
period January 1979 to June 1985 gave 104 articles
having microteaching as a major content descriptor.
Surveying this recent literature gave us three
general impressions about the current state of
microteaching. These impressions concerned its
continued growth, its flexibility in application and
the progress being made towards understanding the
microteaching process.
    In terms of growth the literature shows the
continued spread of microteaching through many
European countries and into Asia. In particular
there are many recent publications from India.
Microteaching is now very firmly established in
teacher education programmes throughout the world.
By far the most impressive finding from the
literature is the flexibility that has been
displayed in applying microteaching to many
different professional groups and institutional
situations. Traill (1979) has suggested that
microteaching has much to offer as a flexible
adaptive procedure. Allen (1980) has pointed to the
flexibility of microteaching as being one of its
main advantages and has given examples of the
different educational levels and the many different

purposes to which microteaching has been applied. Hargie and Saunders (1983b) have cited 16 different groups of professionals with whom various formats of microteaching have been used. McAleese (1983) has reported that, of 821 published microteaching papers examined, some 48% were in areas other than teacher education.

However, despite this spread and the steady publication of articles on microteaching, it is disappointing to have to report that very little progress has been made towards a better understanding of the microteaching process. The great majority of recent publications continue the previous trends of either describing adaptations in specific institutions or reporting findings from experimental studies which have sought to identify optimum conditions for operation. These experimental researches continue to be limited in both aims and design, especially with regard to the assumptions made about the learning gains in microteaching and how to measure them. Hence it is not surprising that their outcomes have not contributed significantly to a better understanding of microteaching. In their review Malley and Clift (1980) concluded that "generalisable links have not been found between specific teaching behaviours and improvements in student learning." They considered that microteaching, although an effective technique, was not clearly superior to other training methods and appeared to be "accepted more on intuition than on empirical evidence." They have suggested that researchers have relied on an inadequate conceptualisation of teacher-pupil relationships to provide the rationale for why microteaching is practised. Similar reservations about research methods have been voiced by Hargie (1982) and about the research evidence by Hewitson (1979), who pointed out that observable performance measures may neglect important affective outcomes. Hewitson also remarked that "the potential of microteaching still appears to be greater than the existing empirical evidence substantiates." These views are now supported by our own studies which point to the range of learning gains that students can make in microteaching, many of which have not been taken into account in process-product research designs. Despite the limited nature of the research evidence about relative effectiveness, many researchers have shown that microteaching continues to be very highly thought of by students and tutors alike.

In only a few developments have efforts been

made to theorise about microteaching and seek
evidence about why and how microteaching actually
works. Hargie and co-workers have continued to
develop their social skills training approach as
'Microtraining' (Hargie, Saunders and Dickson, 1981;
Hargie and Saunders, 1983b). They have defined a
social skill as "a set of goal directed
inter-related social behaviours which can be learned
and which are under the control of the individual"
and point out that an important feature of a social
skill is learning when to use it in terms of timing
and relevance to the prevailing situation. They
have identified a core of social skills that are
widely used and form important parts of the social
interaction of professionals with their students and
clients and also some skills which are specific to
certain professions. The aim of the microtraining
procedure is to improve communicative ability. The
advantage of this approach is that social skills
training is generally applicable to a wide range of
professional groups. In the preparation phase of
microtraining the relevant skills for practice are
identified. The training phase then provides
trainees with skill analysis, skill discrimination,
skill practice and focused feedback sessions.
Analysis is provided in lectures which describe and
examine the skills critically. Discrimination
training takes place in workshops in which videotape
models are viewed and discussed with cueing used to
direct attention to significant aspects of the
model's behaviour. Use of observation schedules and
rating scales helps with the critical analysis of
behaviour components and their effectiveness.
Feedback is provided by the replay of the
videorecordings of the practice sessions with
self-viewing focused by use of rating scales and by
discussions with the tutor. Evaluation takes place
in the following period of fieldwork placement in
which students are encouraged by their tutors to
make a critical evaluation of their skills in
action.
    While the social skills are stressed as
interpersonal relationships, some account is taken
of the effects of the trainee's performance of the
skills on the respondents and this is one of the
criteria that Hargie and Saunders (1983b) considered
important for the construction of model tapes. The
importance placed on skill identification, analysis
and discrimination is an acknowledgement that a
considerable part of the learning in microtraining
is cognitive in nature. Yet Hargie (1982) still

found that "information relating to the cognitive processes which influence the development of teaching skills is at present almost non-existent."

In reviewing microteaching development from 1968 to 1978 McKnight (1980) discussed the complexity of teaching skills and considered Snow's model (1968) of the teaching process to be a useful way of seeing the inter-relatedness of the teacher's values, perceptions, thoughts and actions. Shavelson's revision (1973) of Snow's model considered the teacher's whole value system, attitudes, personality, knowledge and experience as determinants of the teacher's perceptions and actions and hence of the teacher's decision making ability, which Shavelson regarded as the most important teaching skill to which all other teaching skills were related. Decision making as a teaching skill has also been the line of development that McIntyre (1983) has followed in extending his cognitive structures model of microteaching.

McIntyre has pointed out that social skill, as defined by Argyle, includes cognitive processes as well as observable behaviours. He has argued that microteaching had generally been used to train teachers to adopt various desired and generalised patterns of teaching behaviour, whereas the challenge should be to recognise that teaching skills need to be considered as responsive, situation specific and coordinated aspects of the whole teaching ethos and style. He considered that confident, fluent teaching was best achieved through helping students learn to make routine decisions and that microteaching could help, at the cognitive level, by encouraging students to develop their own ideas of what they could realistically achieve. This would enable them to acquire critically evaluated ways of typifying classroom situations which they could use to make routine decisions in seeking to realise their aspirations. Thus he argued "the conception of teaching skill is normative not in relation to specific behaviours but in relation to cognitive processes." McIntyre went on to outline the characteristics of teachers' routine decision making and how students' learning in microteaching could sensitise them to their professional situation and help them develop concepts which then would be available for application in a repertoire of decision making routines for different types of teaching situation. These routines needed to be consistent with the student's long term goals for teaching and

education. McIntyre has suggested that an action
research approach in microteaching could help
students learn how they can most effectively learn
from their teaching experiences.
Although McIntyre has not directly said so,
there is much in this argument which involves the
affective domain as well as the cognitive domain
because the cognitive structures are being built
into the students' belief and value systems and so
involve attitudes and feelings as well as thoughts.
It is the students' belief and value systems which
determine their views of themselves and of the type
of teacher they want to be. Thus McIntyre sees
microteaching as challenging students to develop
those teaching concepts which enable them to
articulate the attitudes to teaching, learning,
interpersonal relationships, classroom climate, etc.
which they would seek to foster in their practice.

UNDERSTANDING MICROTEACHING

We have already used behaviouristic and humanistic
models of teaching, and training and education
orientated models of teacher preparation to account
for tutors' approaches to microteaching. We can
also use these models to suggest reasons for the
relatively unproductive outcomes of microteaching
research and to link the different rationales that
have been proposed for microteaching.

Teaching skills
First of all, behaviourist and humanist teachers
would define 'teaching skill' differently. The
behaviourist would argue that teaching is a very
complex skill indeed and involves a whole hierarchy
of skills and sub-skills that can be practised and
improved. On the other hand the humanist would say
that much that is important in teaching (i.e. the
behaviourist's complex skill) is not about skills at
all and that teaching skills are just the observable
teaching behaviours (the behaviourist's sub-skills).
We can do much to clarify our thinking about
microteaching if we can agree a definition of
teaching skill.
Teaching skills, learning skills, intellectual
skills, social skills, life skills.......skills,
like chips, with everything! Hart (1978) has argued
strongly against the indiscriminate use of the word
'skill' in education because this confuses things
which really are skills with things which are not.

> There is so much talk about skills these days,
> it has become so much a part of the
> stock-in-trade of the would-be
> sharper-than-the-average teacher and
> educationist that it goes unnoticed and
> unheard, like a kind of background hum.
> (p.205)

> Talk about skills is simply an incantation by
> which one creates the illusion that one is
> saying something important about education.
> (p.206)

Accepting the arguments which Hart has
developed and applying them to teaching, we can
define skills as being the technical, observable
behaviours which constitute the teaching act and
which can be adjudged to be performed skilfully. We
would label these behaviours 'performance skills' to
emphasise the point. The other 'complex skills' of
teaching should not be classed as skills because
they are part of the internal cognitive and
affective structures of the teacher - they are, Hart
would argue, human capacities not skills. To label
as skills such cognitive teaching capabilities as
problem solving and decision making and affective
teaching qualities like sensitivity, sincerity and
genuineness is to impoverish them because, to apply
Hart's views on skills to teaching:

> It's true that in order to be able to (teach)
> properly you have to bring something to your
> (teaching). But what you have to bring isn't
> skills; it's yourself. (p.207)

Skills have also been problematic in science
education where 'science skills' has been a rather
ambiguous catch-all term. The Secondary Science
Curriculum Review has suggested in one of its
publications (West, 1984) that a distinction needs
to be made between skills and processes. The Review
has taken a skill to be a specific activity which a
student can be trained to do, and a process as a
rational activity involving the application of a
range of skills.
We can thus distinguish three dimensions which
are involved in using a teaching ability:
performance skill, cognitive processes and affective
learning. All three need to be attended to if a
student is to become competent in using that

154

ability, e.g. explaining. Brown (1978) has analysed
explaining and described workshops on explaining
organised for lecturers in Higher Education. In
studying his materials it is possible to pick out
the three dimensions of this teaching ability,
though they are not explicitly organised as such.
Figure 9.1 shows our suggestions for the objectives
to be attained in each dimension if competent
explaining is to be achieved.

Fig. 9.1: Objectives for competence in explaining

Performance skill

Can present
an explanation
fluently and clearly

Cognitive processes   Competence in explaining

Can construct a   Makes appropriate
rational explanation   decisions about
and can recognise   when to explain
suitable occasions   and gives fluent,
to give explanations   lucid, interesting
                                          explanations

Affective learning

Values explaining
and wishes to give
effective explanations

     This distinction between the performance,
cognitive and affective dimensions of a teaching
ability helps us point to the ambiguous use of the
term 'teaching skill' in much microteaching
research. Often the 'skill' under consideration is
a complex one, yet its operational definition and
measurement takes only performance skill into
account, for example by use of a rating scale. The
inference has to be made by the researcher that a
good performance means that the student appreciates
the value of the skill in its affective dimension
and understands and can apply the skill concept.
Clearly this need not necessarily be the case for
the inter-relationship of the dimensions, although
obviously very close, does not have to be
hierarchically ordered. Thus measurements of
learning gains from microteaching are often very

shallow and hence are invalid indicators of the
total learning that has taken place.

Learning in microteaching

Our descriptive research has indicated that learning
in microteaching is taking place in all three
dimensions and we are arguing for more account to be
taken of the learning that the student makes in the
cognitive and affective dimensions of the teaching
ability. In order to emphasise this point we
present in Figure 9.2 a summary of the potential
learning from microteaching and give indications of
how the various learning outcomes might be assessed.

Fig. 9.2: Potential learning in microteaching.

Learning Dimensions	Learning Situations	Measurement of learning gains
Performance skills	Models to imitate Practice in microlessons Self-viewing feedback	Performance rating scales Tests of pupils' learning
Cognitive processes	Lectures, models and protocols to explain concepts Lesson planning – integrating teaching concepts and subject content Decision making in microlessons Problem solving and analysis in review sessions	Concept testing; e.g. tests, discrimination exerises Problem solving and decision making exercises Evaluation of own and peers' microlessons
Affective learning	Self-confrontation in live microlesson and in self-viewing Discussion of feelings and values in review conferences Sharing of concerns and emotions with peers and supervisor in review conferences	Self-report techniques for attitudes, feelings and relationships e.g. semantic differential, Likert scales Construct elicitation procedures, e.g. interviews, repertory grids

The supervision of microteaching

In discussing the early research on the supervision of microteaching we pointed out that the available evidence was of a conflicting nature. We can now suggest that this was because researchers had not described in detail, nor sought to control, the nature of the supervision provided. We have described how supervision can influence the extent to which each dimension of teaching ability can be emphasised and we found that students made learning gains in those aspects of teaching that their supervisors regarded as important. Students supervised by PCT tutors showed increased ability in teacher self-evaluation, whereas students supervised by TCD tutors developed very positive attitudes to their supervisors' teaching strategy and became very aware of their own progress in understanding teaching and towards becoming a teacher. Students who have different supervisors may have different learning opportunities in microteaching.

The one general finding in the research literature that our studies would support strongly is that students do wish to be supervised. They value supervision and look to their supervisor for experience and expertise, while seeking sufficient freedom of action to experiment with their own approach to teaching. Overall we have found supervision to be a very powerful influence in microteaching.

How can supervisors be helped perform their role in microteaching? We would suggest that this is best accomplished by regarding supervision as teaching. We have provided much case study evidence which we believe supports Dussault's theory of supervision in teacher education. Dussault (1970, p.190) viewed supervision as teaching and has described the type of supervisor-student relationship he considered desirable. He has predicted the nature of changes in students' personality and behaviours which should result from this relationship. Dussault's theory is particularly helpful in showing how the supervisor-student relationship can sensitise the student to the affective learning dimension of becoming a teacher. We have found that Dussault's predictions for cognitive and affective learning gains can be realised, especially in the case of tutors who use a TCD approach which establishes the type of relationship that Dussault advocated.

Advice for tutors in helping students progress in the cognitive processes dimension of pedagogy is

to be found in the work of Stones (1984a). He has
advocated a counselling and pedagogical approach to
supervision whereby students progress by first
grasping the pedagogical concepts and principles.
The students then use these concepts and principles
to appraise teaching activities and go on to apply
them so that ultimately they develop pedagogical
problem solving ability and can "identify, analyse
and solve pedagogical problems in a variety of
conditions." Stones has suggested suitable learning
activities for each of these stages.

Most of the development work in microteaching
has been concerned with the performance skill
dimension of the teaching abilities so there is a
wealth of materials and suggestions available to
provide tutors with any background knowledge that
they may need about this aspect of their
supervision. For example, Brown's book (1975)
contains many examples of performance skill
activities.

It is important that there should not be too
much dissonance between the supervisor's approach
and the rationale for the whole microteaching
programme. Probably the best way of ensuring that
this does not happen is for the staff involved to
agree the rationale that they are using and to spell
this out for students, at least at the level of
broad aims for the programme.

The affective learning dimension

We have argued that microteaching needs to take
account of training in the performance skill
dimension and education in the cognitive and
affective dimensions of the teaching abilities. The
least developed of these in most programmes at
present is the affective dimension and we would like
to offer some suggestions.

In conducting descriptive case study research
we have been deeply involved in relationships with
students and tutors and so have become sensitised to
the affective learning dimension. We have formed
subjective views, which are legitimate products of
case study research because of the illuminative
approach adopted and the triangulation techniques
used to cross-check these views against field diary
notes, systematic observation data, interviews,
students' self-report data and their written answers
to open-ended questions about their learning. We
are very convinced of the value of microteaching as
a beneficial experience for students and we believe
our descriptions of microteaching in action show the

various ways in which students take very large steps forward in their practice of teaching abilities and in their thinking about teaching.

Earlier we pointed to the flexibility of microteaching in terms of its different formats and its use with a wide range of professional groups. We see the main flexibility of microteaching as being the facility with which it can be used to focus on any of the three dimensions of teaching ability as emphasised by the broad aims of the programme and as required for specific students at specific moments in time. This flexibility can be used to help students develop confidence in their teaching abilities, construct their own views on teaching as a professional activity and form their own self-concept as teacher. Microteaching is a powerful technique for helping students change into teachers and not just for improving their performance skills.

How can students be helped develop their affective learning in microteaching? We can point to five sources of ideas and advice. Firstly, Dussault's theory has indicated both the type of supervision that is appropriate and the benefits that should accrue. Secondly, our descriptions of supervision of the Teaching Concept Development style show how the desired supervisory teaching approach and interpersonal relationships can be established. Then again, the use of a small group approach to microteaching is helpful. We have found that the supportive atmosphere of the peer group in review conferences allows students to learn from each other and develop their affective sensitivity. Students moved both early and sensitively to offer each other positive emotional support. Gregory, I. and White, D. (1977) have also described a small group approach. They have claimed that the use of student peer groups in review sessions reduced the severity of self-confrontation, with peers moderating and compensating for tutor criticism.

As well as using an appropriate supervisory style and peer group support to make affective learning one aim of the review conferences, students can be set specific microteaching exercises focused on affective learning about themselves as teachers. Gregory, T.B. (1972) has outlined a microteaching programme which challenges students to face the question, 'What kind of teacher am I?' Gregory believed that microteaching's power to change attitudes was important:

> Microteaching also provides you with a set of
> real, personal teaching experiences that will
> challenge or reinforce many of your conscious
> and unconscious attitudes and values about
> teaching. (p.10)

He has described microteaching tasks for both
the cognitive process and affective learning
dimensions of teaching ability. The affective
dimension tasks stressed the teacher's attitude of
support, positive regard and personal concern for
his pupils and suggested how the teacher could allow
affect to become the subject content of the lesson
in circumstances in which pupils' affective concerns
assumed dominance over their thoughts and
behaviours. The affective tasks were empathising,
respecting, being genuine and communicating
concretely. The aim was that the student should
become sensitive to his pupils' feelings and develop
close relationships with them. The final task was,
'What kind of teacher am I now?' The whole thrust
of the programme was to ensure that "a beginning
teacher has an early encounter with himself as
teacher."

Fifthly, and most importantly we believe,
microteaching itself brings the affective dimension
of teaching to the fore. The core concept of
microteaching which has emerged from our studies is
the rapid, dynamic interchange that the student has
to make between the roles of teacher in the
microlesson and learner in the review conference.
The student in microteaching can be likened to a
spinning coin - now you see one face, now the other,
but the two faces are being blended into the one
person and this involves emotional challenges and
changes in values and attitudes. The competent
teacher is not only a good teacher but also a good
learner. Microteaching brings students to this
issue in a most powerful way. One of the most
important gains of the affective learning dimension
in microteaching is that students come to value, and
can learn to create, relationships which allow them
to learn about and learn from their pupils.

MICROTEACHING: CONSTRUCTS, RATIONALE AND THEORY

We have produced a very different picture of
microteaching to that described in most programmes.
We have revealed the inadequacies of the assumptions
that have often been made about students'

experiences and learning in microteaching. Far from being a simplified, simulated teaching opportunity, microteaching presents a microcosm of all the important issues in learning to be a teacher. The advantage which microteaching offers is the opportunity for sustained self-evaluation through:

- the flexibility to focus on those issues which are important for particular students;

- the consideration of these issues in a more controllable environment than a classroom can provide;

- the close monitoring of progress through review and discussion in which a language of teaching is developed;

- the juxtaposition and hence interaction of the student's roles as learner and teacher, giving opportunities for both cognitive and affective development.

Microteaching constructs

We summarise in Figure 9.3 all the issues that are available for consideration in microteaching. We suggest that there are three broad pedagogical constructs involved: using teaching abilities, learning about teaching and becoming a teacher.

Teaching abilities This construct includes the set of teaching ability concepts on which most microteaching programmes have focused. The major component abilities of teaching , e.g. questioning, reinforcement etc., are selected and education and training activities are provided for each ability. Our review of the literature has reinforced the views of many others that, while there is a fairly broad consensus as to what are the major component abilities, there is not strong research evidence to link good performance of these abilities to effective teaching. We have been able to suggest some reasons as to why this should be so. Measurement of students' learning gains have been too narrow to be valid. Also, these measurements have tended to be made by observer judgements of satisfactory performance rather than by tests of pupils' learning gains.

Teaching Teaching is an integrated, professional activity concerned with bringing about intentional

161

changes in learners. It involves making decisions
about when to use the various teaching abilities and
how to integrate them together into the teaching act
in order to provide conditions which facilitate
learning. This involves knowing the particular
pupils concerned, their interests and needs, and
having realistic expectations of their learning
capabilities. The complex interaction of teaching
and learning comes to be construed as a two way
process in which teaching and learning are taking
place in both directions. Pupils not only learn
from teachers but also teach teachers.

Becoming a teacher This involves the development of
the student's self-concept as teacher. Growing
self-confidence, self-esteem and understanding of
teaching enable the student to come to regard
himself as a teacher. A reconstruction process
takes place with the formation of appropriate
cognitive structures and affective values and
attitudes which will eventually act as the major
influences shaping the student's view of teaching
and influencing his decision making, use of teaching
abilities and perceptions of their effects.

Fig. 9.3: A framework for learning in microteaching

 Pedagogical constructs

   Teaching abilities
   Teaching
   Self-concept as teacher

 Dimensions and levels of learning

 Performance skill
   - practises component behaviours
   - demonstrates in a practice exercise
   - uses in a global skills teaching situation

 Cognitive processes
   - recalls information about...
   - has the concept of...
   - can apply the concept to...

 Affective learning
   - accepts...
   - is willing to...
   - gains satisfaction from...
   - values...

These constructs and dimensions are very
inter-related, but are not hierarchically ordered,
so it is not necessary to consider them in a set
sequential manner. Any starting point will soon
necessitate consideration of the other constructs.
The performance skill, cognitive process and
affective learning dimensions of teaching abilities
are also not hierarchically ordered. What can be
hierachically ordered is the depth of consideration
to which each dimension of teaching ability can be
taken and Figure 9.3 includes suggestions as to what
these levels might be. We have used Stones and
Anderson's (1972) suggestions for levels of
cognitive processes and Horne's (1980) suggestions
for levels of affective learning, adding another
level (values...) from Krathwohl's et al. (1956)
taxonomy for the affective domain. The steps
suggested for acquisition of a performance skill are
those commonly found in microteaching programmes.

Microteaching rationale

This framework of potential learning in
microteaching indicates the issues to be addressed
in deciding the rationale for any particular
microteaching format. Many existing formats do
present a structure which can be logically justified
within this framework, albeit being very limited in
the range of issues they address. Figure 9.4
compares the models of microteaching that have been
adopted by tutors at the New University of Ulster
with the established approaches that have been
described in our reviews earlier in this chapter and
in Chapter One. The constructs and dimensions which
each approach includes are listed in order of the
emphasis which we consider the approach gives to
them.
While a rationale for a microteaching programme
does provide a logical statement of purpose and a
justification in terms of the principles applied, it
can only lead to research of the descriptive,
evaluative type which explores the rationale in
operation. We agree with Hargie (1982) that more
evaluative research in the illuminative style is
needed to continue the process of eliciting the
constructs of microteaching. In this respect Bussis
et al (1976) have pointed to the need to penetrate
"beyond surface curriculum" in the study of teaching
in order to elicit constructs and their technique of
indepth interviewing has proved to be very
beneficial in our research.

Fig. 9.4: Rationales for microteaching

Established approaches	N.U.U. tutors' approaches	Constructs emphasised	Dimensions emphasised
Stanford component skills model	not used	teaching abilities	performance skills, cognitive processes
Turney et al. component skills approach	problem solving for teaching skills	teaching abilities, teaching	cognitive processes, performance skills
Hargie et al. social skills training	not used	teaching abilities, teaching	cognitive processes, performance skills
Guelcher et al. dynamic skills approach	problem solving for teaching practice	teaching, teaching abilities	cognitive processes, performance skills
McIntyre et al. cognitive structures approach	teaching concept development – learning experiences	teaching, self as teacher, teaching abilities	cognitive processes, performance skills
Gregory, encounters with teaching	teaching concept development – relationships	self as teacher, teaching, teaching abilities	affective learning, cognitive processes

From rationale to theory

In order to move on eventually from descriptive, evaluative research to experimental research, a theory of microteaching is needed to provide a basis on which to make and test predictions. Stones (1984b) has argued for the advancement of research in pedagogy through the teacher's conception of self as both theorist and practitioner, the teacher's 'theory' being the body of ideas he brings to the planning of his teaching and to its subsequent appraisal, and the 'practice' being what he actually does. In the process of improving this practice the teacher is testing and extending the theory he is using so that every teaching encounter involves exploration of the relationship between human learning and practical teaching. This idea of developing personal theory through 'investigative pedagogy', as Stones calls it, certainly fits with much of what we have described as happening to students in their microteaching. Indeed this could be the central tenet of microteaching; it uses teaching abilities as the surface curriculum to encourage students to explore their personal theories for teaching.

Any theory of microteaching needs to incorporate theories of teaching, training and behaviour modification, education and cognitive and affective learning. It also needs to take into account the special opportunity that microteaching affords to learn through self-confrontation in a fast feedback, quick turnaround environment. The behaviour modification aspect is available from the original Stanford conception of microteaching which McDonald (1973) has described and which Cooper (1980) has reaffirmed as "training, not education." Both McDonald and Hargie and Saunders (1983) have pointed to Bandura's social learning theory (1971) as providing a suitable source for behaviour modification theory within microteaching. Suggestions upon which the cognitive learning theory for microteaching can be built have been offered by McIntyre et al. (1977) in their cognitive structures model and by McIntyre (1983) in focusing on decision making as the fundamental cognitive process that microteaching can help students develop. Models for the role of decision making in teaching have been developed by Shavelson (1973, 1976) and Shavelson and Stern (1981) have proposed a model of teachers' judgements and pedagogical decisions as a heuristic for organising and conducting research on teaching. They have distinguished planning and interactive types of decision making and their model of interactive decision making regards teachers' main concern during teaching as being to maintain the flow of activity. Although affective learning in microteaching has been the most neglected aspect in practice, a suitable theory is well developed. Dussault's theory of supervision as teaching can not only be applied to the supervisor's role but can also be applied to the student's affective learning.

The main attraction of using McIntyre's, Shavelson's and Dussault's ideas to build theory is that they do take account of the teaching and self as teacher constructs as well as the teaching abilities. An affective learning theory can suggest how values, attitudes and emotions can be fostered in order to create a predisposition to act. The cognitive learning theory can provide reasons for acting so that decisions about which teaching ability to use and when to use it can be made. The behaviour modification theory can suggest how to act. It is a feature of the flexibility of microteaching that all these avenues are available for exploration. Thus microteaching can contribute in a number of ways to the process whereby students reconstruct themselves as teachers and we see the overall theory of microteaching being essentially constructivist in type.

Microteaching provides an excellent opportunity for students to develop their personal model of teaching by linking their performance with their underlying assumptions and personal theory. Personal construct psychology can help us understand how such explorations can be fostered. Pope and Keen (1981) have applied Kelly's personal construct theory (1955) to education and teacher education. They have argued that teachers need to become adaptive, personally viable and self-directing and that such self-direction and self-organisation can only come about if the individual explores his viewpoints and purposes and keeps them under review. The student needs to reflect on the way he construes teaching and the tutor needs to be able to elicit and to respond to the variety of personally relevant issues held by the student. Our descriptions of students and tutors at work have shown how microteaching can supply many of the conditions favourable for a 'personal construct development' approach to learning to teach. Microteaching can reveal students' own views and purposes, can enable students to identify their own shortcomings, and can encourage them to rethink their ideas, set their own goals, evaluate learning in terms of its usefulness to them and, above all, take responsibility for their own learning. A very flexible technique indeed!

A final word

> Microteaching currently has the same promise, and the same danger, that newly devised research and training techniques have always had; the promise of opening up entirely new avenues, perspectives and alternatives to human exploration; the danger of locking in too early on a first alternative which arose purely out of chance and convenience. (Allen and Ryan, 1969, Preface iii)

This quotation has been frequently cited by researchers (e.g. Perlberg, 1976; Gregory and White, 1977; Malley and Clift, 1980) to warn that prematurely set limits could impede a training technique which was still evolving. Our researches have identified some of the "new avenues, perspectives and alternatives" which Allen and Ryan anticipated microteaching would have to offer. We hope that we have been able to point readers in the direction of broadening its applications and developing its theoretical foundations.

APPENDIX A

The Microteaching Review Conference Interaction
Analysis System

The original system, McGarvey (1975), was altered by
Swallow (1984) to allow analyses to be made from
audio-recordings and to increase the number of
problem solving and interaction indices that could
be derived from the interaction matrix. The main
alteration was that the four categories identifying
the utterances of the individual students in the
group were replaced by two categories which just
indicated that a change of student speaker was
taking place. It is Swallow's adaptation of MRCIAS
that is described here.

CONTENT DIMENSION CATEGORIES

1. Structuring
All administrative and procedural comments e.g.
directing and leading procedures which set the
context for discussion by launching or halting
interaction.

2. Teaching skill under focus
The particular teaching skill to be practised in the
microlesson under review; talk about the skill, its
performance in the microlesson, and future
application.

3. Other teaching skills and behaviours
All references to other specific skills, global
skills and other aspects of the student teacher's
behaviour in the microlesson.

4. Lesson organisation and structure
All considerations of the microlesson structure as
planned and as performed, e.g. discussion of the
lesson objectives, lesson plan, etc.

5. Lesson subject content
The subject matter of the lesson, its sequencing, accuracy, suitability, etc.

6. Lesson materials and aids
Discussion of aids, apparatus, etc. used in the microlesson.

7. Pupils' characteristics and behaviours
All talk about the microclass and individuals within it. Includes more general references to pupils' behaviours, e.g. sociological and psychological perspectives.

8. Discipline and control
Classroom management; discussion of good examples or problems observed in the microlesson.

9. Preparations for next week's lesson
Discussion about lesson plan, content materials and aids for next week's microlesson.

10. Preparations for next week's skills
Discussion about the teaching skill which is to be practised next week. Plans for other skills which need to be further practised next week.

11. The microteaching system
The operation and organisation of the microteaching system, e.g. the objectives of microteaching and the review conference, the length of the lessons, the timetable, etc.

12. Other talk
All other talk, including non-task orientated remarks and social exchanges.

13. Silence
Each separate pause estimated to be longer than three seconds. No attempt is made to estimate the length of silences.

14. Non-codable talk
Inaudible remarks and situations of confusion, e.g. two people talking at once.

Appendix A

PROBLEM SOLVING AND VERBAL INTERACTION DIMENSION CATEGORIES

1. **Tutor gives information**
All supervisor talk which provides information, e.g. factual comments, instructions, structuring procedures and directions, explanations of a teaching skill, etc.

2. **Tutor gives analysis**
Supervisor statements which are classed as opinion, analysis or evaluation. Statements of praise or criticism made by the tutor.

3. **Tutor gives suggestion**
Supervisor statements which give advice or offer suggestions.

4. **Tutor asks for information**
Tutor questions asking for a factual or descriptive reply.

5. **Tutor asks for analysis**
Tutor questions which ask the student to give an opinion, judgement, analysis or evaluation.

6. **Tutor asks for suggestion**
Tutor questions which ask the student to offer advice or suggest improvement, modification, different approach, etc.

7. **Tutor accepts, responds**
Supervisor utterances which respond to student talk by accepting or using the student's ideas, e.g. repeating, rephrasing, confirming, extending the student's comments. As the supervisor brings his own ideas into use the coding switches to categories 1, 2 or 3.

8. **Tutor other talk**
All other supervisor talk, e.g. comments which are not task orientated, comments which help build or disrupt the supervisory relationship, social remarks, etc.

9. **A student talks**
No attempt is made to identify individual students.

10. **A different student talks**
This category is used when one student's remarks follow immediately after those of another student.

Appendix A

11. Silence
As in the content dimension.

12. Non-codable talk
As in the content dimension.

CODING PROCEDURES

1. In the first replay of the recording the content
dimension is categorised and the length of total
elapsed time is noted using a stop watch. Since the
content dimension is relatively easy to do, the
observer has the opportunity to familiarise himself
with the group behaviours and identify the speakers'
voices and the student whose microlesson is being
reviewed. The recording is replayed a second time
and the problem solving and verbal interaction
dimension is coded.

2. Coding in from the viewpoint of the observer who
infers the meaning of verbal behaviour from the
recipient's point of view and from the context of
sequentially related behaviours.

3. All thought units are coded, as in the manner of
Weller (1971), following Bales (1950). This unit is
the smallest segment of verbal behaviour which
conveys a complete simple thought. Simple sentences
of subject and predicate are scored as one unit.
Compound sentences joined by "and", "but", etc. are
broken down into their simpler parts, each of which
is scored separately. Complex sentences ordinarily
contain more than one unit, particularly if
adverbial clauses are involved, e.g. "when...
then..."; "if... then..." and "because...". Noun
clauses and adjectival clauses are generally not
treated as separate units. A series of predicates
following a single subject is regarded as separate
units when each one constitutes a new item of
information. These grammatical rules serve only as
guide lines. The general context of discussion will
often indicate a thought unit for sentence
fragments, phrases and even single words.

4. When an individual is making an extended
utterance which is punctuated by encouraging grunts
and words from another member of the group, e.g.
"Uh-huh", these interruptions are not coded unless
they break the flow of the first person's talk.
Similarly, attempted interruptions which are not

accepted by the speaker, who continues with his discourse, are not counted as thought units.

5. Coding of the interactive dimension always starts and ends with code 11 (silence). This is to facilitate the matrix presentation of the data.

INTERACTION MATRIX

A Flanders' type interaction matrix is derived by placing one tally in the appropriate cell for each sequential pair of units coded, with the first number of the pair indicating the row and the second the column. Thus for the codings 1,5 a tally is placed in the fifth cell of the first row. The sequence 1,5,5,9,7 results in tallies in cells 1,5;5,5;5,9;9,7.

Appendix A

Areas within the matrix that are of particular interest for the interpretation of the group interaction are identified by the letters A to G:

Area A denotes extended tutor talk concerned with telling or lecturing.
Area B describes the tutor's questioning behaviour.
Area C denotes the extent of the tutor's response in accepting students' views.
Area D describes the extent of other supervisor talk.
Area E indicates the amount of extended student-student interactions, without tutor involvement.
The F column shows how the students react to the tutor.
Area G denotes the tutor's reactions to the students.

PROBLEM SOLVING AND INTERACTION INDICES

1. Group Indices (3)

1.1. Tutor Talk Ratio:
Sum of Columns 1 to 8 / Sum of Columns 1 to 12

1.2. Student Talk Ratio:
Sum of Columns 9 and 10 / Sum of Columns 1 to 12

1.3. Tutor-Student Talk Ratio:
Tutor Talk Ratio / Student Talk Ratio

2. Tutor Indices (12)

2.1. Tutor Statement Indices (4)

2.1.1. Tutor Statement Ratio:
Sum of Columns 1, 2 and 3 / Sum of Columns 1 to 8
     The proportion of tutor talk which may be categorised as 'tutor tells' or 'tutor gives', relative to the total tutor talk.

2.1.2. Tutor Information Statement ratio:
Column 1 total / Sum of Columns 1, 2 and 3
     This index quantifies the proportion of tutor talk about teaching, i.e. task-orientated value free talk which neither expresses a tutor's opinion (usually praise or criticism) as tutor analysis, nor offers particular advice as tutor suggestion.

2.1.3. Tutor Analysis Statement Ratio:
Column 2 total / Sum of Columns 1, 2 and 3
    This ratio indicates the extent of tutor
utterances which express judgement, expressed as a
proportion of the total tutor information
statements.

2.1.4. Tutor Suggestion Statement Ratio:
Column 3 total / Sum of Columns 1, 2 and 3
    This ratio indicates the extent to which the
tutor offers particular advice and suggestions for
improvement as part of his total information
statements.

2.2. Tutor Questioning Indices (4)
2.2.1. Tutor Questioning Ratio:
Sum of Column 4, 5 and 6 / Sum of Columns 1 to 8
    This index describes the tutor's whole
questioning behaviour as a proportion of the total
number of tutor talk units.

2.2.2. Tutor Information Question Ratio:
Column 4 total / Sum of Columns 4, 5, and 6
    This ratio describes the use of Category 4,
requests for information, as a proportion of the
total tutor questioning behaviour.

2.2.3. Tutor Analysis Question Ratio:
Column 5 total / Sum of Columns 4, 5 and 6
    This ratio identifies the proportion of the
tutor's questions which ask students for their
opinions and evaluations about their own and others'
teaching.

2.2.4. Tutor Suggestion Question Ratio:
Column 6 total / Sum of Columns 4, 5 and 6
    This ratio identifies the proportion of tutor's
questions asking students to synthesise alternatives
as to how they might do it differently.

2.3. Additional Tutor Interaction Indices (4)

2.3.1. Tutor Response Ratio:
Column 7 total / Sum of Columns 1 to 8
    This ratio indicates the use of Category 7,
tutor acceptance and response to student talk,
expressed as a proportion of the total tutor talk.

2.3.2. Tutor Acceptance-Response Ratio:
Area G3 / Total Area G
    The total area G represents tutor utterances

following student talk. Of the total area, only the
sub-area G3 refers to that student-tutor interaction
which may be classified as the tutor accepting and
responding to the students. Thus the ratio Area G3
/ Total Area G gives a sensitive indicator of
tutors' skill in encouraging students to talk about
their own experiences and feelings.

2.3.3. Tutor Indirect-Direct Ratio:
Sum of Columns 4 to 8 / Sum of Columns 1, 2 and 3
        This ratio indicates the tutor's use of
indirect and direct behaviours. Indirect behaviours
involve collaborative problem solving which can be
interpreted by the supervisee as evidence of
personal consideration. Direct behaviours exclude
the supervisee from problem-solving, the
conversation being controlled by the supervisor who
gives the evaluations.

2.3.4. Tutor Extended Talk Ratio:
Sum of Areas A, B, C and D / Sum of Columns 1 to 8
     This index indicates the extent of continuous
tutor talk expressed as a proportion of the total
tutor talk.

3. Student Indices (2)

3.1. Student-Student Interaction Ratio:
Sum of Areas E2 and E3 / Total Area E
     This index indicates the extent of student to
student interactions.

3.2. Student Extended Talk Ratio:
Area E1 / Sum of Columns 9 and 10
        This ratio quantifies the proportion of
extended talk by students as they articulate and
elaborate their own ideas and feelings about
teaching.

Student Relationship Inventory

McGarvey, J.E.B. and Harris, J.E., 1977

Introduction
Below are listed a variety of ways a person may feel
about or behave towards others. Please consider
each statement with reference to the present
relationship between yourself and your supervising
tutor in microteaching.

Instructions
Read each statement carefully and then choose the
code number which expresses how strongly you feel
that it is true or is not true in this relationship.
Ring the appropriate number at the end of each
statement. Please respond to all the statements.
5 = Yes, I strongly feel that this is true
4 = Yes, I feel it is true
3 = I feel that is partly true, and partly untrue
2 = No, I feel that it is not true
1 = No, I strongly feel that it is not true

1. I respect them as persons.
2. I want to be aware of how they feel about
   things.
3. I feel at ease with them.
4. I really like them.
5. I understand their words but do not know how
   they actually feel.
6. Whether they are feeling pleased or unhappy with
   themselves does not change the way I feel about
   them.
7. I am inclined to put on a role or front with
   them.
8. I do feel impatient with them.
9. I am nearly always sensitive to exactly what

they are experiencing.

10. Depending on their actions, I have a better opinion of them sometimes than I do at other times.
11. I feel that I am a real and genuine person with them.
12. I appreciate them personally.
13. The way I feel about them doesn't depend on their feelings towards me.
14. It bothers me when they ask or talk about certain things.
15. I feel indifferent to them.
16. I usually sense how they are feeling.
17. I would like them to be persons of a particular kind.
18. When I speak to them I nearly always can say freely just what I am thinking or feeling at that moment.
19. I find them rather dull and uninteresting.
20. What they say or do sometimes arouses feelings in me that prevent me being sensitive to them.
21. Whether they criticise or show appreciation of me does not (or would not) change my feeling toward them.
22. I care for them.
23. I like them in some ways, while there are other things about them I do not like.
24. I do feel disapproval of them.
25. I can tell what they feel and think, even when they have difficulty in saying it.
26. My feeling toward them stays about the same; I am not in sympathy with them one time and out of patience with them at another.
27. Sometimes I am not at all comfortable with them but we go on, outwardly ignoring it.
28. I put up with them.
29. If they are impatient with me I generally get annoyed or upset too.
30. I am able to be sincere and straight-forward in whatever I express with them.
31. I feel friendly and warm toward them.
32. I ignore some of their feelings.
33. My liking or disliking of them is not altered by anything that they say about themselves.
34. At times I just don't know, or don't realise until later, what my feelings are with them.
35. I value my relationship with them.
36. I appreciate just how their experiences feel to them.
37. I feel quite pleased with them sometimes and then they disappoint me at other times.

38. I feel comfortable to express whatever is in my mind with them, including any feelings about myself or about them.
39. I don't like them as people.
40. Whether they are in good spirits or bothered and upset does not cause me to feel any more or less appreciation of them.
41. I can be quite openly myself in my relationship with them.
42. Somehow they irritate me.
43. At the time I am not aware how touchy or sensitive they are about some of the things we discuss.
44. Whether they are expressing "supportive" thoughts and feelings, or "critical" ones, does not affect the way I feel towards them.
45. There are times when my outward response to them is quite different from the way I feel underneath.
46. At times I feel contempt for them.
47. I am aware of their feelings.
48. Sometimes they seem to me more worthwhile than they do at other times.
49. I truly am interested in them.
50. I often respond to them rather automatically, without taking in what they are experiencing.
51. I don't think that anything they say or do really alters the way I feel toward them.
52. What I say to them would often give a wrong impression of my full thoughts or feelings at the time.
53. I feel affection for them.
54. I feel there are things we don't talk about that are causing difficulty in our relationship.

Scoring

Positive items: 1, 2, 3, 4, 6, 9, 11, 12, 13, 16, 18, 21, 22, 25, 26, 30, 31, 33, 35, 36, 38, 40, 41, 44, 47, 49, 51, 53.

Negative items: 5, 7, 8, 10, 14, 15, 17, 19, 20, 23, 24, 27, 28, 29, 32, 34, 37, 39, 42, 43, 45, 46, 48, 50, 52, 54.

The scoring is reversed for negative items and the scores for all items are added to give a total score.

APPENDIX C

The Self-Concept As Teacher Scale

McGarvey, J.E.B. and Harris, J.E., 1977

Introduction

The purpose of this inventory is to explore how the
various aspects of microteaching help students
develop as teachers. The following statements are
designed to help you describe yourself in terms of
your feelings and views of yourself as a student
teacher in the microteaching lesson and review
conference. Please respond to them as if describing
yourself to yourself. The responses are not an
objective measure of performance but give a guide to
how you see yourself now. They are not used for
assessment and are entirely confidential.

Instructions

Read each statement carefully and then choose the
code number that represents your feelings and view
of yourself now. Ring the appropriate number at the
end of each statement. Please respond to all the
statements.

5 = Completely true (of me and how I see myself)
4 = Mostly true
3 = Partly true and partly false
2 = Mostly false
1 = Completely false

1. I find it easy to get on with my supervisor.
2. I look on each microteaching session as an
   opportunity to improve my skills.
3. I get confused during my microlesson.
4. I am nervous about being recorded in
   microteaching.
5. I find the supervisor's advice and criticism
   helpful.
6. I am eager to improve my teaching skills.

179

7. I can find solutions to the problems that arise during my teaching.
8. Watching my recorded performance reduces my self-confidence.
9. The supervisor shares my problems.
10. I find it hard to talk about my problems with others in the review group.
11. I cannot behave naturally in front of the cameras.
12. I find it hard to talk with the supervisor about my own lesson.
13. I'm not interested in what other members of my group say about my lesson.
14. I am looking forward to my next microteaching lesson.
15. I do not understand what is going on most of the time during my microlesson.
16. I believe that microteaching gives me valuable experiences.
17. I feel dominated by my supervisor.
18. I feel left out of things in my review group.
19. I feel I can learn from observing a recording of my own lesson.
20. I feel in control of what goes on when I'm teaching.
21. I feel inhibited by the technology of microteaching.
22. I try to understand the point of supervisor comments about my microlesson.
23. I would prefer to work alone rather than with a group of students.
24. I can tell the difference between an important and an unimportant event in the classroom.
25. I would prefer it if my group could review and discuss the videotape of our lessons without supervision.
26. I find it easy to get on with the other students in my group.
27. I give up too easily when things get tough in microteaching.
28. I find the microteaching environment artificial.
29. I regard my supervisor as an examiner.
30. I feel that my group works as a team.
31. My standard of teaching compares well with that of the other students.
32. I feel the presence of the cameras makes the microteaching situation unreal.
33. The supervisor encourages me to develop my own confidence.
34. I'm reluctant to ask the other students in my group for advice.

Appendix C

35. I want to be a success at microteaching.
36. I feel restricted in my teaching methods by having to teach in front of the cameras.
37. The supervisor makes valuable comments about my microlesson.
38. I find the suggestions that others in my group make about my teaching helpful.
39. I do not feel in control of what happens during my lesson.
40. I am easily discouraged when problems arise in my microteaching.
41. I would find it easy to approach my supervisor for extra help.
42. The children in my microclass usually take over from me.
43. I would prefer to do microteaching without supervision.
44. I prefer not to take part in discussions when lessons are being reviewed.
45. The other members of my group appear to value my contributions to discussion.

Scoring

Subscale 1, Motivation (5 items):
Positive items - 2, 6, 16, 19, 35.

Subscale 2, Competence (10 items):
Positive items - 3, 7, 20, 24, 31.
Negative items - 15, 27, 39, 40, 42.

Subscale 3, Microteaching Context (8 items):
Positive items - 14
Negative items - 4, 8, 11, 21, 28, 32, 36.

Subscale 4, Supervision (12 items):
Positive items - 1, 5, 9, 22, 33, 41.
Negative items - 12, 17, 25, 29, 37, 43.

Subscale 5, Peer Group (10 items):
Positive items - 26, 30, 38, 45.
Negative items - 10, 13, 18, 23, 34, 44.

The scoring is reversed for negative items and the scores for appropriate items are added to give the sub-scale and total scale scores.

The Student Post Teaching Questionnaire

Swallow, D.J., 1984

Purpose and design

The purpose of the instrument is to identify the number and range of issues that students are concerned or pleased about immediately following the teaching of their microlesson and before their review conference. It also provides an analysis of the students' responses in terms of the quality of their lesson experience self-confrontation, thereby giving a description of one aspect of the students' learning in microteaching. The questionnaire invites free responses to an open-ended question, this design taking into account three important criteria:

1. Students' responses need to be openly self expressed to avoid
(a) contamination of the ensuing review conference by cueing students on to aspects of the lesson taught that may be followed up in the review conference,
(b) contamination of the analysis of the range and depth of self-confrontation by cueing students on to teaching issues.

2. Students are to be encouraged to write distinctly in expressing their immediate reactions to their teaching as dictated by their post teaching self-confrontational experiences.

3. Students are to be encouraged to differentiate their issues of satisfaction and concern in order to assist the process of analysis.

Appendix D

Administration
Students are given an unlimited time period
immediately after teaching their microlesson to
record their views and feelings about their
teaching.

**How do you feel about the microlesson you have just
taught?**

1. Please write down on the sheets provided those
   reactions (impressions, perceptions, evaluations,
   feelings about your progress, etc.) which pleased
   or dissatisfied you about your lesson.

2. Specify clearly (and in detail, if necessary) the
   point you are making.

3. Please take a new paragraph for each separate
   comment you make. Do not combine in one
   paragraph, points which you feel can be
   differentiated. Number your paragraphs
   sequentially (1), (2), (3), etc.

Analysis of responses

Swallow (1984) has provided a detailed Coding Manual
which was used to train two independent coders who
had not been involved in the development of the
analysis system. The inter-coder agreement
coefficients obtained after this training were found
to be very satisfactory. The Coding Manual explains
the system with the aid of a large number of
examples from the students' responses.
    The coding unit is the thematic statement. The
total number of themes identified by the student is
counted and each theme is analysed in terms of the
dimensions: substantive category, self-critique,
thinking in explaining and self-application.

1. Substantive category

The theme is classified as:

1.1 Learning experiences

1.1.1 The teaching skill under focus that week
      (Where the student identifies the programme of
      weekly skills as an aspect of microteaching
      requiring consideration, this is coded under
      the relevant sub-category of 1.2)
1.1.2 Teaching behaviours, other than the skill

under focus
1.1.3 The lesson
1.1.4 The pupils

1.2 The microteaching system and organisation

1.2.1 The supervisor
1.2.2 Tutor attendance during teaching
1.2.3 Assessment
1.2.4 Reviewing the lesson
1.2.5 Editing the videotape
1.2.6 Immediate/delayed feedback
1.2.7 Student peers
1.2.8 The weekly skill
1.2.9 Microteaching technology
1.2.10 The microclassroom
1.2.11 The pupils
1.2.12 Lesson time
1.2.13 Weekly/biweekly teaching
1.2.14 Order in which students teach
1.2.15 Lesson planning

1.3 Me (affect and self-regard) only
This category is reserved for themes where the focus
of attention is on 'myself and how I feel'.

2. Self-critique

Three aspects of self-critique are recorded:

2.1 Value weighting
The theme is categorised as to whether it contains
no value weighting (i.e. is just informative
description), positive critique, negative critique,
or balanced critique. The latter is applied when a
respondent uses both positive and negative critique
within the one statement.

2.2 Self-affect
Students' expressions of what they are feeling about
the experience indicates the subjectivity associated
with personalised expressions of 'myself as
teacher', in contrast to an impersonal cognitive
account of the lesson. Statements are categorised
as to whether 'self-affect' is present or absent.

2.3 Self-progress
All progress statements, whether expressed in
positive or negative terms are considered to be
important in that they relate directly to how the
students are learning from microteaching.

Appendix D

Statements are categorised as to whether or not they contain expressions of self-progress.

The analysis of these three aspects of self-critique is then used to classify each statement into one of five categories, as summarised by the figure: Structuring self-critique.

Structuring self-critique

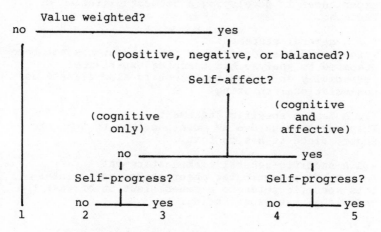

i.e. 1. No value weighting
     2. Affect, no; progress, no
     3. Affect, no; progress, yes
     4. Affect, yes; progress, no
     5. Affect, yes; progress, yes

3. Thinking in explaining

This dimension records the degree of analysis expressed within the statement.

3.1 Non-relational statements are exemplified in simple descriptive reporting or unsubstantiated opinions and assertions.

3.2 Relational statements embody a reason-giving explanation. A thematic statement may be made up of more than one unit of thought, linked together as dealing with the one issue or theme.

Each unit of thought is read and the question 'Why?' asked. If the answer is provided by any of the other units of thought, then the statement contains relational thinking.

4. Self-application

Each statement is coded as belonging to one of three categories. This dimension has been called self-application, it being considered that categories 1, 2 and 3 illustrate the increasing application of the student's own specific experiences in developing a conceptualisation of his teaching.

4.1 A general statement
This provides evidence that the student has not been prepared to analyse his teaching experience (especially so if the statement is also classed as non-relational thinking).

4.2 A lesson specific statement
This may be regarded as more penetrating than the above, since it has context.

4.3 A specific-general linked statement
This takes a particular observation, and relates this specific point to a generalisation of what the individual was experiencing.

BIBLIOGRAPHY

ALFONSO, R.J., FIRTH, G.R. and NEVILLE, R.F.,
(1975), Instructional Supervision: A Behavior
System, Allyn and Bacon, Boston.

ALLEN, D.W., (1980), "Microteaching: a personal
view", British Journal of Teacher Education, Vol.6,
No.2, pp.147-151.

ALLEN, D.W. and RYAN, K., (1969), Microteaching,
Addison Wesley, Reading, Massachusetts.

APPLEBEE, A.N., (1976). "Microteaching, component
skills and the training of teachers: an evaluation
of a research and development project", British
Journal of Educational Technology, No.7, Vol.7,
pp.35-44.

ARGYLE, M., (1967), The Psychology of Interpersonal
Behaviour, (1st edn.), Penguin, Harmondsworth,
Middlesex.

ARGYLE, M., (1969a), Social Interaction, Methuen,
London.

ARGYLE, M., (1969b), "Social skills training in
education", Paedagogica Europaea, Vol.5, pp.72-79.

BAKER, H.P., (1970), "Film and videotape feedback: a
review of the literature", Report Series No.53,
Contract No. OEC-6-10-108, Research and Development
Center for Teacher Education, Texas University,
Austin.

BALES, R.F., (1950), "Interaction process analysis:
a method for the study of small groups", Addison
Wesley, Reading, Massachusetts.

Bibliography

BANDURA, A., (1971), Social Learning Theory, General
Learning Press, New York.

BARRETT-LENNARD, G.T., (1962), "Dimensions of
therapist response as causal factors in therapeutic
change", Psychological Monographs, Vol.76, No.43,
pp.1-36.

BERLINER, D.C., (1969), Microteaching and the
Technical Skills Approach to Teacher Training,
Technical Report, No.8, Stanford University,
California.

BIGGE, M.L., (1982), Learning Theories for Teachers,
Harper and Row, New York.

BLOOM, B.S. (Ed.), Engelhart, M.D., Furst, E.J.,
Hill, W.A. and Krathwohl, D.R., (1956), Taxonomy of
Educational Objectives: The Classification of
Educational Goals, Handbook 1: Cognitive Domain,
David McKay, New York.

BLUMBERG, A., (1968), "Supervisory behavior and
interpersonal relations", Educational Administration
Quarterly, Vol.4, No.2, pp.34-45.

BLUMBERG, A., (1970), "Supervisor-teacher
relationships: a look at the supervisory
conference", Administrators Notebook, Vol.19, No.1,
pp.1-4.

BLUMBERG, A., (1974), Supervisors and Teachers: A
Private Cold War, McCutchan Pub. Co., Berkeley,
California.

BORG, W.R., KELLEY, M.L., LANGER, P. and GALL, M.,
(1970), The Mini Course: A Microteaching Approach to
Teacher Education, Macmillan, Beverley Hills,
California.

BORTON T., (1970), Reach, Touch and Teach: Student
Concerns and Process Education, McGraw-Hill, New
York.

BROWN, G.A., (1973), "The effects of training upon
performance in teaching situations", unpublished
D.Phil. thesis, New University of Ulster, Coleraine.

BROWN, G.A., (1975a), "Microteaching: Research and
Developments", in CHANAN, C. and DELAMONT, S.,
(Eds.), Frontiers of Classroom Research, National

188

Bibliography

Foundation for Educational Research, Slough.

BROWN, G.A., (1975b), Microteaching: A Programme of Teaching Skills, Methuen, London.

BROWN, G.A., (1975c), "Teaching and microteaching: models, rationale and programme", Education for Teaching, Vol.98, pp.71-79.

BROWN, G.A., (1975d), "Some case studies of teacher preparation", British Journal of Teacher Education, Vol.1, pp.71-85.

BROWN, G.A., (1978), Lecturing and Explaining, Methuen, London.

BROWN, G.A. and ARMSTRONG, S., (1975), "More about microteaching", Trends in Education, Vol. 1, pp.49-57.

BROWN, G.A. and McGARVEY, J.E.B., (1975), "The processes of supervision in microteaching", Research Intelligence, Vol.1, No.2, pp.49-53.

BRUSLING, C., (1972), "Microteaching", School Research Newsletter, Gotenburg School of Education, Sweden.

BRUSLING, C., (1974), Microteaching - A Concept in Development, Almqvist & Wiksell, Stockholm, Sweden.

BUSSIS, A.M., CHITTENDEN, A.E. and AMAREL, M., (1976), Beyond Surface Curriculum. An Interview Study of Teachers' Understandings, Westview Press, Boulder, Colorado.

COHEN, S. and HERSH, R., (1972), "Behaviorism and humanism; a synthesis for teacher education", Journal of Teacher Education, Vol.23, No.2, pp.172-176.

COMBS, A.W., (1969), Florida Studies in the Helping Professions, University of Florida Press, Gainesville.

COMBS, A.W., (1972), "Some basic concepts for teacher education", Journal of Teacher Education, Vol.23, No.3, pp.286-290.

COMBS, A.W., (1977), "A humanist's view", in COMBS, A.W., POPHAM, W.J. and HOSFORD, P.L., pp.53-57.

189

COMBS, A.W., POPHAM, W.J. and HOSFORD, P.L., (1977), "Behaviorism and Humanism: A Synthesis?", Educational Leadership, Vol.35, No.1, pp.52-63.

DAYTON, C.M., (1970), The Design of Educational Experiments, McGraw-Hill, New York.

DEARDEN, G. and LAURILLARD, D., (1977), "Illuminative evaluation in action: an illustration of the concept of progressive focussing", Research Intelligence, Vol.3, No.2, pp.3-7.

DOLL, W.E., Jr., (1979), "A structural view of curriculum", Theory into Practice, Vol.28, No.5, pp.336-348, December.

DUSSAULT, G., (1970), A Theory of Supervision in Teacher Education, Teachers College Press, Teachers College, Columbia University, New York.

FINLAYSON, D., (1975), "Self-confrontation: a broader conceptual base?", British Journal of Teacher Education, Vol.1, No.1, pp.97-103.

FLANDERS, N.A., (1970), Analysing teaching behaviour, Addison Wesley, Reading, Massachusetts.

FOSTER, J., HEYS, T. and HARVEY, J., (1973), "Microteaching: A review and a study of the effects of microteaching upon teaching effectiveness", Forum of Education, Vol.32, No.2, pp.100-141.

FULLER, F.F. and MANNING, B.A., (1973), "Self-confrontation reviewed: a conceptualization for video playback in teacher education", Review of Educational Research, Vol.43, No.4, pp.469-528.

GIBBS, I., (1973), "Some responses of students at the New University of Ulster to microteaching", unpublished M.A. thesis, The New University of Ulster.

GOLDHAMMER, R., (1969), Clinical Supervision: Special Methods for the Supervision of Teachers, (1st Edn.), Holt, Rinehart and Winston, New York.

GOLDHAMMER, R., ANDERSON, R.H. and KRAJEWSKI, R.J., (1980), Clinical Supervision: Special Methods for the Supervision of Teachers, (2nd Edn.), Holt, Rinehart and Winston, New York.

Bibliography

GREGORY, I. and WHITE, D., (1977), "A small group approach for microteaching programmes", British Journal of Teacher Education, Vol.3, No.3, pp.243-251.

GREGORY, T.B., (1972), Encounters with Teaching, a Microteaching Manual, Prentice-Hall, Englewood Cliffs, New Jersey.

GRIFFITHS, R., (1972), "The role of the tutor in microteaching supervision: a survey of research evidence", University of Stirling, Department of Education, June.

GRIFFITHS, R., (1974), "The contribution of feedback to microteaching technique", University of Stirling, paper presented at the APLET/NPLC Microteaching Conference, Reading, January.

GRIFFITHS, R., (1975), "The training of microteaching supervisors: a review", British Journal of Teacher Education, Vol.1, pp.11-15.

GRIFFITHS, R., (1976), "Preparing tutors for microteaching supervision", Educational Media International, Vol.1, pp.11-15.

GRIFFITHS, R., (1977), "The emergence of a cognitive perspective in microteaching", Educational Studies, Vol.3, No.3, pp.191-196.

GUELCHER, W., JACKSON, T. and NECHELES, F., (1970), "Microteaching and teacher training - a refined version", Chicago University, ERIC ED 050 017.

HAMILTON, D., JENKINS, D., KING, C., MACDONALD, B. and PARLETT, M., (Eds.), (1977), Beyond the Numbers Game: A Reader in Educational Evaluation, Macmillan, Basingstoke, Hampshire.

HARGIE, O.D.W., (1980), "An evaluation of a microteaching programme", unpublished Ph.D. thesis, Ulster Polytechnic, Jordanstown.

HARGIE, O.D.W., (1982), "Research paradigms and theoretical perspectives in microteaching", British Journal of Teacher Education, Vol.13, No.1, pp.76-82.

HARGIE, O.D.W., DICKSON, D.A. and TITTMAR, H.G., (1978), "Mini-teaching: an evaluation of the microteaching format", British Journal of Teacher Education, Vol.4, No.2, pp.103-118.

HARGIE, O.D.W. and MAIDMENT, P., (1978), "Discrimination training and microteaching: implications for teaching practice", British Journal of Teacher Education, Vol.9, No.2, pp.87-93.

HARGIE, O.D.W. and MAIDMENT, P. (1979), Microteaching in Perspective, Blackstaff Press, Belfast.

HARGIE, O.D.W. and SAUNDERS, C.Y.M., (1983a), "Individual differences and social skills training", in ELLIS, R. and WHITTINGTON, D., (Eds.), New Directions in Social Skills Training, Croom Helm, London.

HARGIE, O.D.W. and SAUNDERS, C.Y.M., (1983b) "Training professional skills", in DOWRICK, P.W. and BRIGGS, S.J., (Eds.), Using Video: Psychological and Social Applications, Wiley, Chichester.

HARGIE, O.D.W., SAUNDERS, C.Y.M. and DICKSON, D., (1981), Social Skills in Interpersonal Communication, Croom Helm, London.

HART, W.A., (1978), "Against skills", Oxford Review of Education, Vol.4, No.2, pp.205-216.

HEWITSON, M., (Ed.), (1979), Research into Teacher Education: the Practical Teaching Skills, ERDC Report No.19, Australian Government Publishing Service, Canberra.

HORNE, S.E., (1980), "Behavioural objectives in the affective domain: a new model", British Educational Research Journal, Vol.6, No.2, pp.189-196.

HILLIARD, F.H., (1971), "Theory and practice in teacher education", in HILLIARD, F.H. (Ed.), (1971), pp.33-54.

HILLIARD, F.H., (1971), Teaching the Teachers: Trends in Teacher Education, Allen and Unwin, London.

HIRST, P.H., (1971), "What is teaching?", Journal of Curriculum Studies, Vol.3, pp.5-18.

Bibliography

KALLENBACH, W.W. and GALL, M.D., (1969), "Microteaching versus conventional methods in training elementary intern teachers", _Journal of Education Research_, Vol.63, No.3, pp.136-141.

KELLY, G.A., (1955), _The Psychology of Personal Constructs_, Vols.1 and 2, W.W. Norton, New York.

KELLY, G.A., (1970), "A brief introduction to personal construct theory", in BANNISTER, D., (Ed.), _Perspectives in Personal Construct Theory_, Academic Press, New York.

KORAN, J.J., (1969), "Supervision: an attempt to modify behaviour", _Educational Leadership_, Vol.26, No.7, pp.54-57.

KRATHWOHL, D.R., BLOOM B.S. and MASIA, B.B., (1956), _Taxonomy of Educational Objectives, Book 2: Affective Domain_, David McKay Co.Inc., New York.

MACLEOD, G., (1976a), "Students' Perceptions of Their Microteaching Performance", unpublished Ph.D. thesis, University of Stirling.

MACLEOD, G., (1976b), "Self-confrontation revisited", _British Journal of Teacher Education_, Vol.2, No.3, pp.219-222.

MACLEOD, G., (1977), "A descriptive study of students' perceptions of their microteaching performance", in MCINTYRE, D., MACLEOD, G. and GRIFFITHS, R., (1977), _Investigations of Microteaching_, Croom Helm, London, pp.194-204.

MACLEOD, G., GRIFFITHS, R. and MCINTYRE, D., (1977), "The effects of differential training and of teaching subject on microteaching skills performance", in MCINTYRE, D., MACLEOD, G. and GRIFFITHS, R., (1977), _Investigations of Microteaching_, Croom Helm, London, pp.142-153.

MACLEOD, G. and MCINTYRE, D., (1977), "Towards a model for microteaching", _British Journal of Teacher Education_, Vol.3, No.2, pp.111-120.

MALLEY, J.I. and CLIFT, J.C., (1980), _A Review and Annotated Bibliography of the Microteaching Technique_, Royal Melbourne Institute of Technology, Melbourne.

McALEESE, W.R., (1983), "Skills training and self-confrontation applications in different settings", in TROTT, A. and GIDDINS, L., (Eds.), Improving Efficiency in Education and Training, Kogan Page, London.

McALEESE, W.R. and UNWIN, D., (1971), A selective survey of microteaching", Programmed Learning and Educational Technology, Vol.3, No.1, pp.10-21.

McALEESE, W.R. and UNWIN, D., (1973), "A Bibliography of Microteaching", Programmed learning and Educational Technology, Vol.10, No.1, pp.40-54.

McDONALD, F.J., (1973), "Behaviour modification in teacher education", in THORESEN, C.E., (Ed.), Behaviour Modification in Education, National Society for the Study of Education Yearbook No.72, Part 1, University of Chicago Press, Chicago.

McDONALD, F.J. and ALLEN, D.W., (1967), "Training effects of feedback and modelling procedures on teaching performance", Report No. BR-5-1030, Contract No. OEC-6-10-078, Stanford University.

McGARVEY, J.E.B. and WILLIAMS, I.W., (1978), "Microteaching", in ASHMAN, A., HILLS, P.J., MOYES, R.B. and PLATTS, C.V., (Eds.), Educational Techniques in the Training of Science Teachers, The Chemical Society, London.

McINTYRE, D., (1983), "Social skills training for teaching: a cognitive perspective ", in ELLIS, R. and WHITTINGTON, D., (Eds.), New Directions in Social Skill Training, Croom Helm, London.

MCINTYRE, D., MACLEOD, G. and GRIFFITHS, R., (1977), Investigations of Microteaching, Croom Helm, London.

McKNIGHT, P.C., (1980), "Microteaching: development from 1968 to 1978", British Journal of Teacher Education, Vol.6, No.3, pp.214-227.

MEDEIROS, D.C., WELCH, D. and TATE, G.A., (1979), "Humanistic teacher education: another view", Educational Leadership, Vol.36, No.6, pp.434-438.

MEDLEY, D.M. and MITZEL, H.E., (1963), "Measuring classroom behaviours by systematic observation", in GAGE, N.L., (Ed.), Handbook of Research on Teaching, Rand McNally, Chicago.

194

Bibliography

MERRILL, M.D., (1968), "Instructional design - A new emphasis in teacher training", Educational Horizons, Vol.47, No.1, pp.9-20.

MILLAR, C. and MCINTYRE, D., (1977), "The analysis of students' evaluations of observed teaching", in McINTYRE, MACLEOD and GRIFFITHS, Investigations of Microteaching, Croom Helm, London, pp.79-99.

MORRISON, A. and MCINTYRE, D., (1969), Teachers and Teaching, Penguin, Harmondsworth, Middlesex.

MORRISON, A. and McINTYRE, D., (1972), (Eds.), Social Psychology of Teaching, Penguin, Harmondsworth, Middlesex.

NASH, R.J., (1970), "Commitment to competency: The new fetishism in teacher education", Phi Delta Kappan, No.52, pp.240-243.

NASH, R.J., (1972), "In the summer of '71: an experiment in teacher education", Journal of Teacher Education, Vol.23, No.1, pp.11-20.

NASH, R.J. and AGNE, R.M., (1971), "Competency in teacher education: a prop for the status quo?", Journal of Teacher Education, Vol.22, No.2, pp.147-156.

OLIVERO, J.L., (1970), Microteaching: Medium for Improving Instruction, Merrill, Columbus, Ohio.

PAI, Y. and KRUEGER, (1979), "Accountability at what price?", Journal of Teacher Education, Vol.30, No.4, pp.20-21.

PARRY, G., (1977), "A bibliography of supervision", Programmed Learning and Educational Technology, Vol.14, pp.134-141.

PARRY, G. and GIBBS, I., (1974), "A bibliography of supervision", Programmed Learning and Educational Technology, Vol.11, pp.97-111.

PEREIRA, P. and GUELCHER, W., (1970), "The skills of teaching: a dynamic skills approach", Chicago University, Graduate School of Education, ERIC ED 049 162.

PERLBERG, A., (1976), "Microteaching - present and future directions", Educational Media International,

Vol.2, pp.13-20.

PERROTT, E., (1972), "Course design and
microteaching in the context of teacher training",
Paper presented at the International Microteaching
Symposium, University of Tubingen, W. Germany,
Conference Report: Centre for New Learning Methods,
University of Tubingen.

PERROTT, E., (1976), "Changes in teaching behaviour
after participating in a self-instructional
microteaching course", Educational Media
International, No.1, pp.16-25.

PERROTT, E., (1977), Microteaching in Higher
Education: Research Development and Practice,
Research into Higher Education Monographs, No.31,
Society of Research into Higher Education, Guilford.

POPE, M.L. and KEEN, T.R., (1981), Personal
Construct Psychology and Education, Academic Press,
London.

POPHAM, W.J., (1977), "Behaviorism as a bugbear", in
COMBS, A.W., POPHAM, W.J. and HOSFORD, P.L.,
pp.57-62.

ROGERS, C.R., (1957), "The necessary and sufficient
conditions of therapeutic personality change",
Journal of Consulting Psychology, Vol.21, pp.95-103.

ROGERS, C.R., (1959), "A theory of therapy,
personality and interpersonal relationships, as
developed in the client-centred framework", in KOTH,
S. (Ed.), Psychology: A study of a Science, Vol.lll,
Formulations of the Person and the Social Context,
McGraw-Hill.

ROWLEY, G.L., (1976), "The reliability of
observational measures", American Educational
Research Journal, Vol.13, No.1, pp.51-59.

SALSBURY, R.E., Jr., (1969), "A study of the
feasibility of the Washington State
University-Bellevue Public Schools Career Teacher
Project", Doctoral dissertation, Washington State
University.

SCHAEFER, R.J., (1970), "Teacher education in the
United States of America", Prospects in Education, A
Quarterly Bulletin, Vol.1, No.2, pp.37-42.

Bibliography

SCOTT, W.A., (1955), "Reliability of content analysis: The case of nominal scale coding", Public Opinion Quarterly, 1955, Vol.19, pp.321-325.

SEIDMAN, E., (1969), "A critical look at microteaching", in BABIN, P., (Ed.), (1969) Student's Guide to Microteaching, Center of Cybernetic Studies, Ottawa University, Ontario.

SHAVELSON, R.J., (1973), "What is the basic teaching skill?", Journal of Teacher Education, Vol.14, pp.144-151.

SHAVELSON, R.J., (1976), "Teachers' decision making", in GAGE, N.L., (Ed.), The psychology of Teaching Methods, University of Chicago, Chicago.

SHALVESTON, R.J. and STERN, P., (1981), "Research on teachers' pedagogical thoughts, judgements, decisions and behaviour", Review of Educational Research, Vol.51, No.4, pp.455-498.

SHEPARDSON, R.D., (1972), "A survey (utilizing the Delphi Method) to assess and objectively display the arguments for and against developing a performance-based teacher education program", Journal of Teacher Education, Vol.23, No.2, pp.166-171.

SHIVELY, J.E., VAN MONDFRANS, A.P. and REED, C.L., (1970), "The effect of mode of feedback in microteaching", Paper presented at AERA Annual Meeting, ERIC ED 037 391.

SHROUT, P.E. and FLEISS, J.L., (1979), "Intraclass correlations: uses in assessing rater reliability", Psychological Bulletin, Vol.86, No.2, pp.420-428.

SNOW, R.E., (1968), "Heuristic teaching", Third annual report, Stanford Center for Research and Development in Teaching, pp.78-84.

SOARE, A.T. and SOARE, S.M., (1968), "Self-perceptions of student teachers and the meaningfulness of their experience", Journal of Teacher Education, Vol.19, pp.187-191.

SOARE, A.T. and SOARE, S.M., (1974), "Self-perception as affective dimensions of student teaching", Paper presented at American Educational Research Association annual meeting, Chicago.

ST. JOHN-BROOKS, C. and SPELMAN, B., (1973), "Microteaching", Trends in Education, Vol.31, pp.14-19.

STONES, E., (1984a), Supervision in Teacher Education, a Counselling and Pedagogical Approach, Methuen, London.

STONES, E., (1984b), Psychology of Education: a Pedagogical Approach, Methuen, London.

STONES, E. and ANDERSON, D., (1972), Educational Objectives and the Teaching of Educational Psychology, Methuen, London.

STONES, E. and MORRIS, S., (1972), Teaching Practice, Problems and Perspectives, Methuen, London.

SWALLOW, D.J., (1984), "Case studies of construct systems and processes in microteaching", unpublished D. Phil. thesis, New University of Ulster, Coleraine.

TERHART, E. and DRERUP, H., (1981), "Knowledge utilization in the science of teaching: traditional models and new perspectives", British Journal of Educational Studies, Vol.XXIX, No.1, pp.9-18.

THORESEN, C.E., (Ed.), (1973), Behavior Modification in Education, Seventy-second Yearbook of the National Society for the Study of Education, Part 1, University of Chicago Press, Chicago.

TITTMAR, H.G., HARGIE, O.D.W. and DICKSON, D.A., (1977), "Social skills training at Ulster College", Programmed Learning and Educational Technology, Vol.14, No.4, pp.300-304.

TRAILL, R.D., (1979), "Microteaching and the development of practical teaching competencies", in HEWITSON, M., (Ed.), Research into Teacher Education: the Practical Teaching Skills, ERDC Report No.19. Australian Government Publishing Service, Canberra.

TRAVERS, R.M.W., (1975), "Empirically based teacher education", The Educational Forum, Vol.39, No.4, pp.417-433.

Bibliography

TURNER, R.L., (1975), "An overview of research in teacher education", in RYAN, K., (Ed.), Teacher Education, The Seventy-Fourth Yearbook of the National Society for the Study of Education, Part II, The University of Chicago Press, Chicago, Illinois, pp.87-110.

TURNEY, C., CLIFT,J.C., DUNKIN, M.J. and TRAILL, R.D., (1973a), Microteaching: Research, Theory and Practice, Sydney University Press, Sydney.

TURNEY, C., CAIRNS L., WILLIAMS, G., and HATTON, N., (1973b), Sydney Micro Skills. Series I Handbook. Reinforcement, Basic Questioning, Variability, Sydney University Press, Sydney.

TURNEY, C., CAIRNS, L.G., WILLIAMS, G., HATTON. N. and OWENS, L.C., (1975), Sydney Micro Skills - Explaining, Introductory Procedures and Closure, Advanced Questioning, Sydney University Press, Sydney.

TURNEY, C., and CAIRNS, L.G., (1976a), Sydney Micro Skills - Classroom Management amd Discipline, Sydney University Press, Sydney.

TURNEY, C., THEW, D.M., OWENS, L.C., HATTON, N. and CAIRNS, L.G., (1976b), Sydney Micro Skills - Guiding Small Group Discussion. Small Group Teaching and Individualised Instruction, Sydney University Press, Sydney.

TURNEY, C., RENSHAW, P. and SINCLAIR, K.E., (1977), Sydney Micro Skills - Learning and Fostering Creativity, Sydney University Press, Sydney.

WAETJEN, W.B., (1963), "Self-concept as learner scale", in ARGYLE, M. and LEE, V., (Eds.), Social Relationships, Open University Press, Bletchley, Bucks., 1972.

WAGNER, A.C., (1973), "Changing teacher behaviour: a comparison of microteaching and cognitive discrimination training", Journal of Educational Psychology, Vol.64, No.3, pp.299-305.

WAIMON, M.D., BELL, D.D. and RAMSEYER, G.C., (1972), "The effects of competency-based training on the performance of prospective teachers", Journal of Teacher Education, Vol.23, No.2, pp.237-245.

Bibliography

WAIMON, M.D. and RAMSEYER, G.C., (1970), "Effects of video feedback on the ability to evaluate teaching", Journal of Teacher Education, Vol.21, No.1, pp.92-95.

WALKER, B.S. and LITTLE, D.F., (1969), "Factor analysis of the Barrett-Lennard relationship inventory", Journal of Consulting Psychology, Vol.16, No.6, pp.516-521.

WARD, J.H. Jr., (1963), "Hierarchical grouping to optimize an objective function", American Statistical Association Journal, Vol.58, pp.236-244.

WARD, B.E., (1970), A survey of Microteaching in Secondary Education Programmes of all NCATE Accredited Colleges and Universities, Memorandum No.70, Stanford Center for Research and Development in Teaching, Stanford.

WATTS, D., (1978), "The humanist approach to teacher education: a giant step backwards?", Educational Leadership, Vol.36, No.2, pp.87-90.

WELLER, R.H., (1971), Verbal Communication in Instructional Supervision, Teachers' College Press, Columbia University.

WEST, R.W., (1984), (Ed.), Towards the Specification of Minimum Entitlement: Brenda and Friends, Secondary Science Curriculum Review, Schools' Council, London.

WILSON, J., (1975), Educational Theory and the Preparation of Teachers, National Foundation for Educational Research, Slough.

WOLFE, D.E., (1970), "A study to determine the feasibility of including the direct experiences of microteaching and team teaching, and interaction analysis training in the pre-service training of foreign language teachers", Doctoral dissertation, Ohio State University.

YOUNG, J.I., BLAINE, N.L. and RICHARDS, D.R., (1971), "The effect of controlled variables in microteaching", ERIC ED 050 557.

YOUNGMAN, M.B., (1979), Analysing Social and Educational Research Data, McGraw-Hill, London.

200

INDEX

Index

Index

Index